NEW ZEALAND TRAGEDIES

on the Track

Tangiwai and other Railway Accidents

There was no age barrier when it came to posing for a photograph in front of derailed locomotive La 313 at Hou Hou near Hokitika in December 1910.

114

NEW ZEALAND TRAGEDIES

on the Track

Tangiwai and other Railway Accidents

Geoff Conly · Graham Stewart

Grantham House
New Zealand

Also by Geoff Conly
J. J.'s Dunedin
The Shock of '31

Watties: The First Fifty Years
Tarawera: The Destruction of the Pink and White Terraces
Piet's Eye in the Sky
New Zealand Pohutukawa

Also by Graham Stewart
Tangiwai Disaster
The End of the Penny Section
When Trams were Trumps in New Zealand

Previous Page: A Boer War troop train derailed near Invercargill on 26 March 1900. The locomotives were V114 (left) and U194.

First Published 1986
Revised edition 1991

GRANTHAM HOUSE PUBLISHING
P.O. Box 17-256
Wellington 5
New Zealand

ISBN 1 86934 008 6

Edited by Anna Rogers
Typeset by Wordset Enterprises Limited, Wellington
Designed by Bookprint Consultants Limited, Wellington
Printed in Hong Kong through Bookprint Consultants Limited, Wellington

Acknowledgements

Help with research, and advice, is particularly appreciated from Mr Alan C. Bellamy of Tauranga, Mr Harry Campbell and Mr Les Veale, both of Napier, and Tom McGavin of Wellington. Others who helped with expert advice include Messrs Gordon Duthie (Locomotive Supervisor, Napier) and C. M. O. Martin (of Napier Operations).

Acknowledgement is made to the late W. W. Stewart for the many illustrations from his private collection; to Mr Jack McClare and Mr Harry Campbell, for photographs; and to the late Derek Cross for his picture of the Tangiwai bridge the day before disaster struck.

Photographs of the Tangiwai disaster, many taken by Graham Stewart, are from the photographic library of Wilson and Horton Ltd.

Our thanks to Vere Dodds of *Reader's Digest*, Sydney, and to Mr Jim Eades, the owner of the cover painting.

Many hands were needed to right this derailment caused by a washout near Pigeon Bush in the Wairarapa in the late 1890s. The salvage team had time to stop work and hold a pose while this scene was captured by a photographer with a camera and tripod, on a slow but reliable glass plate. The locomotive was Fa 182.

CONTENTS

The result of a head-on collision near Matamau in Hawke's Bay in April 1896. The locomotive was J 235.

INTRODUCTION

This book seeks an insight into the more notable steam train accidents in New Zealand and the reasons why many of these mishaps happened.

For everybody, this is history, for steam has long gone as the prime means of locomotive power. The image, though, remains. Those magnificent giants which pulled the Main Trunk expresses, polished, shiny proud, pulsating and hissing steam, seemed invincible. Yet some were unfortunate, being derailed, overturned, squeezed in collisions, lost in fog — the record is in the pages which follow.

Some passengers, as with some train crew, were unlucky, but most walked away from the accident scene, occasionally because of miraculous escapes. A casual change of seat, that a passenger was standing instead of sitting at the time of the crash, the angle at which the carriages were travelling at the moment of disaster — these and a score or so other occurrences, simple in themselves but fraught with momentous possibilities, played their part in grim tragedy. To one or other, some passenger has owed his or her life.

With the passing of the years the shock and impact fades and these accidents become part of our history. But they must not be ignored. The Tangiwai disaster of Christmas Eve 1953 overshadows all the others in popular conception, but whenever people died or were badly injured there were others to mourn and sympathise.

The accident rate on New Zealand Railways was dropping sharply in the years before and while steam was being phased out, to the point where riding in a railway carriage (or a commuter train) was among the safer forms of travel. Some part of this gain was due to the lessons learnt from the accident toll.

As a result New Zealand Railways now has much better operating conditions; track curvature is better than it was a generation ago, for instance. The old 8 chain curves (160 m) have been modified, gradients are easier, ballasting better, the track more secure through improved standards of track work, visibility improved, drainage better; rerouting avoids unstable country and there are wider cuttings. While motorists can see and appreciate major roading improvements, rail passengers are probably content to know they are getting to their destinations faster, in greater comfort and greater safety! Modern railway operation is a technology of its own, but a price was paid in the long haul from the days when the first steam locomotive operated in New Zealand (in 1863). Part of that price, the costliest toll, is told in these pages.

Mount Ruapehu looms above the train wrecked by the wake of water discharged from the mountain's crater lake.

Mount Erebus 1979 (centre left), Hawke's Bay 1931 (centre right), HMS Orpheus 1863 (lower left), Mount Tarawera (lower right).

Chapter 1

TANGIWAI TRAGEDY THAT STUNNED A NATION

New Zealand's most tragic railway disaster happened on Christmas Eve 1953, when the Wellington to Auckland express plunged into a roaring torrent of lahar floodwater sweeping down the Whangaehu River at Tangiwai. One hundred and fifty-one men, women and children were killed.

Minutes before the express crossed the Whangaehu River railway bridge, a sudden discharge of thousands of tonnes of water from the crater lake of Mount Ruapehu sent a giant 6 m (20 ft) roaring wave on a path of destruction. This great surge of water carried away the massive concrete piers of the railway bridge, wrecked the adjacent road bridge and swept on to smash down three smaller bridges nearer the coast.

At 10.21 p.m. on Christmas Eve the 3 p.m. express from Wellington hurtled in a death plunge from the weakened bridge. Travelling across the plateau at 60–90 km (40–50 miles) an hour, the 145 tonne Ka locomotive flew through the air and almost struck the opposite bank, 35 m (40 yds) away. The five second-class carriages behind crashed into the raging waters. A sixth carriage, the leading first-class car, teetered for a few minutes on the edge of the jagged gap, before following the first coaches into the river.

This was the fifth worst disaster in New Zealand's recorded history and, at the time, the eighth biggest railway disaster the world had known. In a few brief minutes, Tangiwai claimed more victims than the total lost in all other New Zealand railway accidents, the death toll being more than double the losses suffered collectively at Ongarue, Opapa, Ratana, Mercer, Hyde and Seddon.

New Zealand's greatest disaster was the crash of an Air New Zealand DC10 on Mount Erebus, Antarctica, in 1979, in which 257 people died. Next worst was the Hawke's Bay earthquake of 3 February 1931, in which 256 people were killed. The wreck of HMS *Orpheus* on Manukau Bar on 7 February 1863 caused the next highest death toll, with the loss of 181 lives, while 153 perished when Mount Tarawera erupted on 10 June 1886.

Like the Hawke's Bay earthquake — and the Tarawera and Murchison disasters — the Tangiwai accident struck suddenly and without warning, savagely and without mercy.

Only a handful of people knew on Christmas Eve 1953 that, in spite of the dry conditions which had prevailed, the Whangaehu River was in flood.

Daniel Miles Chapman, of Bulls, was driving his passenger bus between Bulls and Turangi along the Desert Road when his radiator boiled. So, with can and billy, he walked from the road through the scrub to the river to get water, and came upon it suddenly, rushing by at his feet — a liquid which looked like pea soup, coloured grey, with black specks in it. Afterwards he wondered if he was the only person in New Zealand who had foreknowledge of the Whangaehu's flooding.

He wasn't. Arthur Cyril Ellis, of Taihape, who was to win a George Medal for his bravery, found his way blocked by floodwaters although no rain was falling and none had fallen on his journey from Taihape to make a Christmas call on his parents at Rangataua, near Ohakune.

He reached the road bridge over the Whangaehu River at Tangiwai to find the decking was well under turbulent yellow water, with only the top rail of the side rails visible. He told his wife and mother-in-law, who were in his truck, what he had seen, backed the vehicle well out of possible danger and then returned with his five-cell torch for a closer look. It was then he saw a light approaching from the direction of the Tangiwai crossing just south of the river.

At first he thought the light was that of a car, and called to his wife accordingly, but then realised it was a train. He had no idea it was the express, and, although he could not see the railway bridge, he had a strong premonition something was wrong. So he ran towards the engine, waving his torch, shouting, trying to warn the driver or fireman.

The ill-fated locomotive Ka 949 which crashed to destruction at Tangiwai hauling the daylight limited north over the twin bridges south of Waiouru, the day before the Tangiwai disaster. Picture by Derek Cross.

As he was to recall,

> I did not know what train, but I realised that with the river in that state it had no chance of crossing the rail bridge. I jumped the railway fence and ran up the embankment. I ran down the middle of the track brandishing my torch and shouting at the top of my voice in an endeavour to attract the attention of the engine driver or fireman. I ran away from the bridge to try and give the crew more room to pull the train up, but it was no use — they just didn't see the torch. I jumped clear and yelled to the driver when the locomotive roared past me about 200 yards from the bridge, but he had no chance of hearing me above the roar of both river and engine. As the train passed I realised for the first time that it was the express. I didn't know the bridge was damaged; I had merely realised that with the flood they could not get across. . .[1]

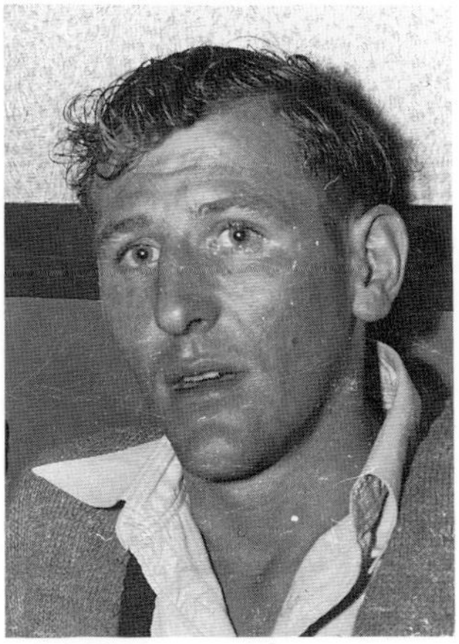

Postal clerk Cyril Ellis resting the day after the disaster. He was awarded the George Medal for bravery in saving passengers from the sixth carriage.

Charles Parker (far left), driver of the express and victim of the disaster. Lance Redman (left), the fireman who perished as the train nose-dived into the river.

Neither driver nor fireman expected trouble.

Ka 949's driver, Charles Parker, was a special grade engine driver with 33 years' service who had been stationed at Taihape since 1938. His fireman, Lance Redman, was born and bred at Taihape and, apart from service in the Armed Forces during the Second World War, had worked trains out of his hometown since joining the locomotive running branch in 1940. Both men were conscientious, efficient and well-respected members of the community.

The Taihape crew was booked to drive the express to Pokaka, 81 km (51 miles) north of Taihape, change there to the southbound express and return to Taihape, where they would be home early in the morning. Home for Christmas Day. Engine driver Parker had wanted to sign off early at Christmas, so had arranged with a colleague to swap duties, but at the last minute the men were told that all locomotive running staff must work the rosters as posted. The holiday season is always a busy period for the railways and Christmas was no exception; swapping shifts would only complicate matters. So on Christmas Eve, Charles Parker's mate who offered to drive the express worked his rostered duty. He survived.

The working timetable stated that the goods train would proceed south to Tangiwai station shortly before the express was due and wait on the station siding until the northbound express passed. As the south goods was running late that evening and was not allowed to delay a passenger train, it was held at Karioi, the first station north of Tangiwai, to allow Parker a good clear run through Tangiwai with the north express. Had the goods train been on time it would surely have suffered the fate of the express.

Before and after — Ka 949 was in top condition before the disaster at Tangiwai left the locomotive a crumpled wreck on the edge of the Whangaehu River.

The engine drawing the express, a 1400 hp monster which had had a complete overhaul only four months previously, was running sweetly. Ka 949 was in top condition, though built at the Hutt railway workshops in 1939.

The composition of the ill-fated express was:

Type of vehicle	Rolling stock number	No. of seats in each carriage	Car letter
Second-class cars	A 1907	56	E
	A 1899	56	D
	A 1915	56	C
	A 1862	56	B
	A 1920	56	A
First-class cars	Aa 1717	29	Z
	A 1887	31	X
	A 1857	31	V
	A 1889	31	W
Van	F 592		
Postal van	Fp 707		

Total weight of train: 467.3 tons.
Total length of train over buffers: 213 m (approx.)

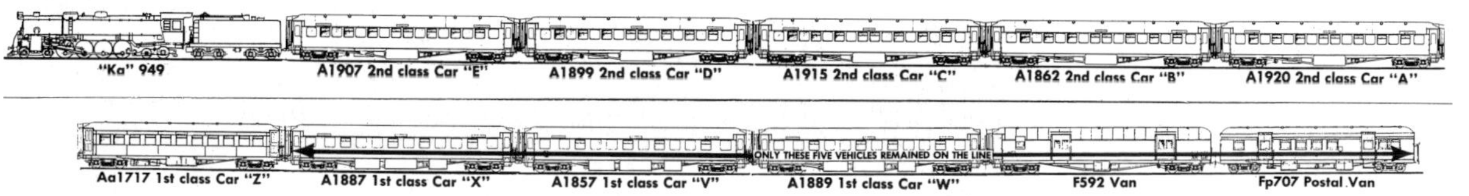

The other players in this tragedy were the passengers. The total number of people on the train was 285, most, in the traditional New Zealand way, taking their annual holidays from Christmas Eve. In families and groups they had sorted themselves through the carriages and had whiled the time away since the 3 p.m. departure from Wellington. Did many of them expect to see the Queen and Duke of Edinburgh after they had arrived in Auckland the next morning? Would Father Christmas visit the excited children aboard the train? What new holiday delights lay in store? What excitement? What adventures?

At Waiouru eight passengers left the train and one boarded, the last stop before the catastrophe. And soon the express was passing through Tangiwai and fast approaching the Whangaehu River bridge, on time, a routine trip in every way except that this was Christmas Eve.

The station agent at Tangiwai, Raymond John Hall, listened as the express sped past about 65 km (40 miles) an hour and noted that the train was being driven more slowly than usual. The driver usually increased his speed as his engine passed through Tangiwai. Hall sat down on his chair, but almost immediately heard a loud roaring noise, which made him jump and look out the window. He could see the four tail lights of the express.

The day before disaster struck. A northbound goods train crossing the Whangaehu River bridge at Tangiwai at 10 a.m. on 23 December 1953.

The giant wave which carried away the Whangaehu River railway bridge was as high as 6 m (20 ft) and it roared with a rolling tongue which could be heard at Waiouru, 9.5 km (6 miles) to the east. This wall of dirty yellow water, tossing boulders and trees as it plunged downriver from Mount Ruapehu, carried away the massive concrete piers and steel girders of the bridge, gave the adjacent road bridge a sharp twist and swept on to smash three other smaller bridges nearer the coast.

So when, half an hour later, the Christmas Eve express from Wellington raced on to the sagging bridge rails there was nothing to support the train. It buckled in the middle, then went twisting down into the torrent. The engine nose-dived off the southern bank and, with a bellowing splash, almost carried to the other bank.

The first carriage went with it. The second carriage reared up into the air, nose first, and took the next three with it. They seemed to telescope one another. The sixth carriage, the first of the first-class coaches, balanced at an angle of 45° with half its

The same scene as that on the opposite page but on the day following the Tangiwai disaster, Christmas Day 1953. The view from the north abutment of the broken bridge shows the wreckage of the Ka locomotive beside a fallen bridge girder in the foreground.

length sloping off the sheared-off rails of the bridge, until it too took its death plunge.

Four of the carriages were minced down to tangled sheet steel and splintered woodwork and the chassis. Only the underframes remained, the rest being torn to pieces by the river. Two carriages survived the somersaulting reasonably well and gave up a good proportion of the survivors, while the last three carriages miraculously remained on the line at the broken end of the bridge, along with the two vans.

Unsuspecting passengers were thrown at the mercy of the torrent. In the darkness survivors clambered or were hauled — wet, plastered with mud and soaked with oil — from the twisted remains. Others, breaking clear, were grasped by the current and carried downstream, some to find a new footing and reach the banks and safety. Others, the unlucky ones, were given no chance; they drowned or were smothered by the thick silt clogging the swollen river. The injured, robbed of the physical capacity to fight for life, went under. And some were swept far downriver to be lost forever in the ocean.

Passengers who survived the Tangiwai tragedy lived ever afterwards with the screams of people trapped in the wrecked carriages. The cries died away as the water rose in the cars, or as they disintegrated. And the survivors, many hurt, most mud or oil stained and almost all in some state of shock, wondered what had happened.

One such passenger was J. A. Blair, of Christchurch, who had been one of a party of four men playing cards in the carriage immediately behind the locomotive. The four later met on the riverbank, marvelling how they had got there. Blair remembered turning two somersaults as his carriage hurtled from the bridge. The car landed on its side, allowing him to crawl through a broken window, only to slip and be caught in the torrent and swept a kilometre (half a mile) downstream before he was able to crawl ashore.

A companion, R. E. Coveny, also of Christchurch and a one-time successful jockey, was flung round the carriage and, when it came to rest, found himself in swirling water up to his chest. He also crawled through a broken window but retained his hold on the uppermost side of the carriage. From there he struggled about 4.5 m (15 ft) to the shore. Both men suffered only bruises and they helped with rescue work until billeted in a house at Karioi.

In the same carriage were Mr and Mrs D. McLean, who lost their belongings but saved their two children. 'I was dozing when, without warning, there was a crash and a terrific sort of plunge,' said Mr McLean afterwards. 'Then there was a sensation of going downhill at terrific speed, as if the train had got away on the spiral. There was a jolt and water started pouring into the carriage, which had listed on to its side.'

The water began to rise, so he tried to break a window before noticing that one behind him had been broken, so he struggled out through it. His son, who had been sitting beside him, was unceremoniously hauled out the same window by his hair. 'I heard my wife calling out and I reached in to help her and our daughter to the roof, where we were assisted by passengers who had already crawled there. I think we are the luckiest family on the train.'

Other passengers experienced a sickening sensation as their carriages fell into the river. 'It must have been a good 50 feet but we were lucky,' said one survivor. 'It fell on its wheels and stayed there. When the carriage hit the bottom the windows all fell open. It was just as well they did, too, though the water poured in.'[2]

Len Wasley, a railway employee, told how, horror-stricken, he awoke from a doze to find himself being tossed about like a cork. 'Then,' he said, 'I felt myself being smothered with water and oil.'[3] Charles Sulenta, a carpenter of Auckland, was with Len Wasley, also in the carriage immediately behind the engine, and he lived because of the carriage hurtling over the top of the engine.

'God knows how we came out of it alive,' he said. He got out by squeezing himself through a window and on to the roof.

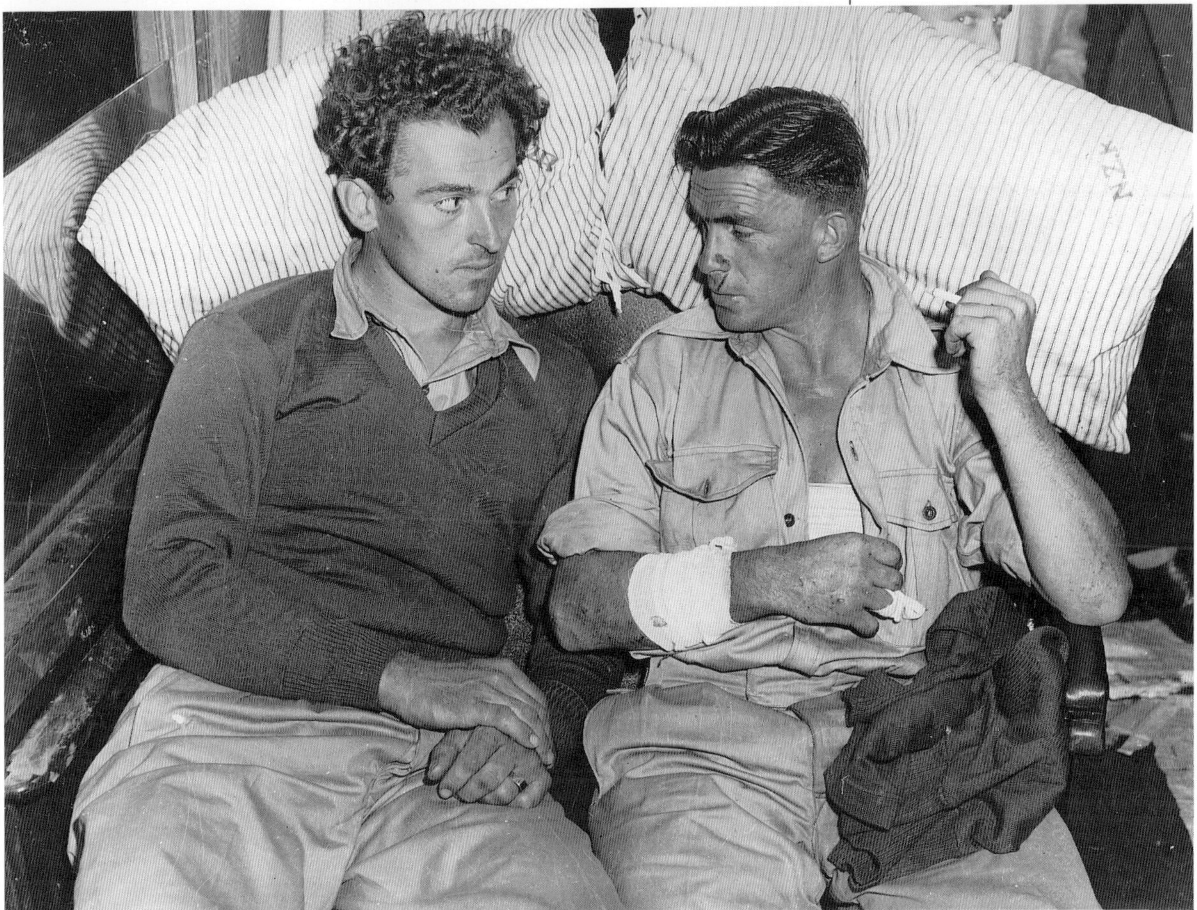

Survivors from the first carriage behind the locomotive, Messrs C. D. Sulenta (left) and L. Wasley, dressed in clothing issued by the Army on their way to Auckland in a relief train. Both gave testimony at the inquiry.

'There was only 9 inches of the carriage sticking above the water . . . We hung on to the roof for half an hour until help arrived and we got ashore. I was covered with oil from the engine from head to foot.'[4] A friend of Charles Sulenta, a Fijian, had gone to the toilet just before the crash. He died.

R. Kyle who, with his wife, was travelling from Wellington to Huntly, was dozing when the accident happened: 'I was shocked into a state of awareness by the crash and vibrations of the carriage. At first I did not realise how bad it was but, when the car trembled, I realised something was wrong. . . . I will never get from my ears the screams of those who were trapped in the carriages in the water.'[5]

He paid tribute to a group of young men from his carriage who, plunging into the water, formed a chain to rescue people who had clambered on to the roof of a carriage. The force of the water was so great they had their clothes stripped from them.

Three young men who found their seats in a first-class carriage occupied when they joined the train obtained accommodation in a second-class coach. Shortly before the accident the guard told them he had got their proper seats for them. They went with him and the move probably saved their lives. The car they had been in plunged into the water. Seventeen-year-old Barbara Mahy, of Whakatane, and her brother John,

John Holman, a passenger on the train, received the George Medal for his part in rescuing 21 people trapped in the sixth carriage.

The shattered remains of Carriage Aa 1717, Car Z, the sixth carriage on the train. This was the only first class coach to crash into the water.

15, were also travelling with first-class tickets in a second-class carriage, second in line from the engine. Just before the train reached Waiouru the guard found them two first-class seats in the last carriage on the train. Also in that last carriage were W. Davis, of Mosgiel, his wife and son Mervyn, on their way to Kaikohe. The jolt they felt seemed like a severe earthquake. When the train stopped they got out, to be stunned by the wreckage scattered below them.

'Horrible, horrible,' was the opinion of Miss J. Smith, of Stokes Valley, who was in the sixth carriage, the only first-class coach to crash into the water. 'We were just sitting talking when there were three enormous jolts. We sat and waited. Then the suspended carriage rolled over and over and all the time water was coming in. I hung on to the luggage rack and I grabbed a man by the hair and pulled his head above the water. I don't know who he was and he won't have known me in the dark.

'When the carriage came to rest on its side we were able to break the windows and someone hauled me on to the roof. One man, Mr John Holman, was particularly brave.

'We were lucky the carriage landed on its side. If it hadn't, we wouldn't have got out.

'Only one person, a girl, did not get out. She was trapped in her seat, when two elderly men were thrown on top of her as the carriage rolled in the water. It was awful.

Another view of Carriage Aa 1717. The coach was cut in two by ropes when a bulldozer righted the car body while searching for victims.

'I suppose we were in the water in the carriage for about three minutes. We waited there till the men made a human chain to get us to the riverbank.'[6]

J. C. Falloon, of Christchurch, thought 'it was the end, this was it, and we were not going to get out of it.

'We heard a roar. It must have been the water. Then we seemed to stop with a bang and with other bangs behind us. I thought we must have hit another train. Then our engine was in the water and our car lurched at an angle. I looked out and there were no cars either before or behind. Then our car went over and we hit the river.

'We must have rolled over half a dozen times. Mud and water poured in. The car was washed about 200 yards down-river, then stuck on a sandbank turned on its side. That's what saved us. I smashed open a window and another chap smashed one further down the car. We pulled ourselves up and held our hands in the air. It seemed we were there about an hour. A man on the bank ran back to get help. I think that's how they got to us.

'When I got out I was with my wife and I was so dazed for a while I didn't know it was her. Just to know we were saved was enough.'[7]

Miss Minnie Dean, of Dargaville, was in Z carriage, sixth from the engine and was falling asleep when disturbed by 'a terrific jolt. I though it was an earthquake. Women screamed. We had stopped and the lights were on. Then we saw the water pushing against the side. The guard came through and told us to get to the back of the train quickly. The lights went out. I was trying to push my way through the carriage when it fell over — quite slowly. It was pitch black and the water was swirling into the carriage above the seats. I remember floating around, touching people, grabbing on things, but not seeming to get anywhere. Then I saw a passenger's hand sticking through one of the windows from the outside and heard a man telling me to hang on. I grabbed the hand but my fingers slipped and I went down and down. When I came up again the hand was still there. This time it grabbed me and someone gave me a shove from underneath.'[8]

'When the water first came into the carriage I remember thinking, "If I have to die I hope it will be quick",' said Miss D. Sutherland, of Palmerston North. Before the accident she and a girlfriend had talked about their new clothes and told each other jokes. 'Someone had given us a chicken to eat at midnight and we had eaten it already.'

When the carriage fell into the water some women had screamed but someone said, 'Get out.' But another voice said, 'Sit still.' There was a cracking sound and the carriage rolled over. Someone broke a window and because she had a torch she was among the first to be helped out on to the side of the carriage. A man took her torch to help others out.

'It seemed an eternity while we sat there. The men from the part of the train that did not go over made a sort of ladder for us. They stood in the water and joined hands. We went across holding onto them.'[9]

While many passengers helped themselves — and others — to safety, the first 'outside' rescuers were on the scene surprisingly quickly. They included forestry workers, Ministry of Works staff, sailors and soldiers. This was hard and distressing work, among what one soldier called 'a shambles. . . I saw the Blitz in London and nothing there tore my heart as this did.'[10]

Soldiers' wives and WAACs from the Waiouru Military Camp formed a voluntary group to provide hot tea and coffee for the rescue squads, whose numbers grew by the hour.

A view from the south bank showing how the heavy locomotive leapt right across the river. In front is the wreckage of the third carriage beside a demolished span of the bridge.

Colin Morgan, of Lower Hutt, standing by the seat he occupied at the time of the crash. He was one of the few survivors from this carriage, A 1915, the third on the train. Colin said he was half asleep, with his pillow propped against the carriage window. All he remembered of the plunge off the bridge was the carriage rolling over and over. When he regained consciousness he was lying draped over a tree high up on the northern bank of the river. He was one of the lucky ones; the torrent had carried him to safety.

An aerial view of the doomed train on the banks and in the bed of the Whangaehu River. The railway line from Waiouru runs from right to left across the middle of the picture. The main highway bridge is at bottom right.

This photograph shows clearly the wrecked and twisted remnants of the express.

In the light of an overcast Christmas Day dawn, the scene at the wreck resembled a mud estuary at low tide. The receding Whangaehu River had left a broad, grey, boggy path and on this and in the swiftly flowing grey river winding through it lay carriages and pieces of carriages, the twisted locomotive and tender, all like so much driftwood.

Of the 80 m (88 yd) railway bridge, only a stubby span on the south side remained. The middle pile, a massive concrete pier weighing many tonnes, had been hurled 68 m (75 yds) downstream. A heavy steel girder lay nearby. The road bridge lay at a drunken angle, water swirling through a 3.5 m (12 ft) break at its southern end. Completely submerged at the height of the flood, its decking was left deep in sand where the water had gone and its trusses were grey with mud and clumps of grasses. Fortunately for rescue workers, the river had subsided almost as quickly as it had risen. At daybreak a giant bulldozer was harnessed up to begin turning wreckage and digging into the soft silt, but long before that, quite soon after the accident, the work of search and rescue had begun.

The first outside helper was postal clerk Cyril Ellis, whose unsuccessful efforts to stop the express meant that he watched the engine nose-dive into the torrent, carrying five carriages with it and leaving a sixth perched perilously on the brink of the bank.

Senior guard William Ian Inglis did not know what had happened until told by Ellis that 'half your train is in the river'.[11] Together they entered the precariously balanced sixth carriage and Inglis went to the front of the car and looked out the door. 'Good God,' he said, 'we have lost five carriages and the engine.'[12] He urged passengers to walk back through the train, but the advice came too late for there was a bang as the back coupling snapped and down the carriage went with all the people in it.

Cyril Ellis still had his five-battery torch and, as the carriage lights failed, he grabbed the rail of the luggage rack.

'She rolled over a couple of times and then came to rest on her side, with the water flowing through. It was wicked. I had a couple of women hanging on to me, but I managed to knock

William Ian Inglis, the guard on the ill-fated train.

out a window with an elbow and my feet,' he said.

With John Holman, of Wellington, Cyril Ellis got everyone out of the carriage, except a girl who had been trapped in her seat with her head under water. She was drowned. 'I cannot explain what we went through, but somehow in the stress of the moment both John and I seemed to have terrific strength.'[13]

With the carriage on its side the water was within about 300 mm (11 ins) of the higher set of windows and with heavy pieces of luggage floating about the task of getting people out in time proved very difficult. Mrs Ellis and her mother watched horror-stricken from the roadway. Not until it was all over did they learn Cyril had joined those whose lives hung in the balance.

Guard Inglis noted there was no movement of the sixth carriage once it had tipped on its side. With help he assisted people through the broken windows. 'I then remember noticing how the water had receded and saw men walking towards the car from the riverbank,' he said. 'They were in water about knee-deep. They formed a human chain to the car and proceeded to take the persons off the car.

'I was among the last to leave and when I left some of the rescue men were on the car. I got off on the river side and the water was just above my ankles.'[14]He then returned to the train and inspected the handbrakes, to find they had been applied.

Arthur Dewar Bell.

Arthur Dewar Bell, who was to receive the British Empire Medal for his courage, saw the disaster happen and promptly went to the rescue of some 15 people, while his wife drove to the New Zealand Forestry Service centre at Karioi. The fire siren was sounded there to bring out all hands and they were taken to the river.

Mrs Bell drove to a forestry camp at Karioi to raise the alarm.

Early on the scene was Constable L. S. Smidt, of Waiouru, who had earlier been puzzled by a roaring noise. He had discussed it with Warrant Officer Yorke, of Waiouru, and the stationmaster, E. J. Kyle, speculating about it being wind in a tree plantation about 6 km north of Waiouru, or the sound of water. He set out to investigate, in a taxi driven by Ross Harrison. About 70 m from the railway bridge they saw the red lights of the rear of the express and the tail lights of two vehicles by the traffic bridge. The sky was overcast and it was very dark, while the water was a raging torrent.

Constable Smidt went straight to car Z — the sixth carriage — and, inside the car, found himself 'up to my thighs in water'.[15] Three people were still in the carriage: John Holman and two other men, with the body of a woman at the far end. He and another man took the body out. Although he was only two or three minutes in the carriage, when he got out there was barely any water at all; it had gone down very suddenly. There had been an ice deposit on the edge of the water, which was more like mud. Boulders could be heard moving in it.

The alert spread to the Army at Waiouru, the Navy at HMNZS *Irirangi*, the Ministry of Works at Waiouru and the police at Taihape, where Senior Sergeant R. Griffith gathered a small party of constables. Other police officers came from as far

The interior of car Z, the only first-class carriage to fall into the river.

The wreckage of car Z as it was left in the bed of the river when the flood receded. This first-class carriage remained poised on the line before falling into the swollen river. All but one of the 22 occupants of this carriage were rescued. Valiant efforts by the rescuers were later appropriately recognised.

This picture shows the nature of the damage to the main highway bridge which crossed the Whangaehu River between Ohakune and Waiouru. Deep scouring occurred at the southern abutment (left). Two carriages were swept by the flood right across the highway, bypassing the bridge, one ending up on an island 2 km (1½ miles) downstream from the railway bridge. Somehow the highway bridge withstood the battering force of the flood and was not carried away completely.

afield as Taumarunui, Stratford and Hawera, although the main early rescue force came from male passengers in the three unscathed first-class carriages at the rear of the train. Their clothing — and many were in their best clothes — was ruined by the thick oil from the tender or the black silt which clogged and coated everything.

Only about two dozen soldiers were on duty when the alarm was sounded at Waiouru Military Camp. Weary troops who had finished duty slapped one another's faces to drag themselves to full wakefulness. Local Post Office exchanges round the district put out mass calls for help, and within minutes trucks, jeeps and private cars were rounding up helpers. Flares, axes, shovels, blankets and all sorts of emergency gear were rushed to the river. Civilians in Waiouru township lent everything they had which could be of use. Shopkeepers threw open their stores. On the other side of the river, at Ohakune, Raetihi, Karioi and the small villages, similar measures were in operation. Forty gangers from Ohakune were mobilised.

While search and rescue staff were concentrated at the wreck, or in search parties downstream, back at Waiouru Camp the staff had begun a round-the-clock toil. Cookhouses baked and prepared enough food and hot drinks to feed the hundreds who were helping, as well as relatives of victims who were coming on the sad journey of identification.

In a gaily decorated hall under bright streamers put up for a children's Christmas party, half-open coffins were laid in orderly rows. At one side was a heart-rending group of white

Twisted seats and silt — all that was left of the fourth carriage, A 1862. The floodwaters had carried this car a long way downstream past the road bridge, shedding the roof and sides down to window-ledge level.

children's coffins, beside them tiny shrouded figures. Behind a yellow screen where a dance band usually played was a sodden silt-covered pile of clothing. A heap of suitcases lay in one corner and beside them a child's rubber ball. Identification was made more difficult because most of the victims' clothes had been torn from them, while correspondence and papers which would normally assist the police had been swept away.

Car headlights were used first to shine down on to the wild scene, which was broken by the gleam of torches as men searched for more survivors. At 11.30 p.m., a little more than an hour after the crash, the Army brought up a diesel generator, four spotlights and a carbon arc searchlight. Sparks flew from arc torches as workers cut through steel in search of lives to save. Steam from the heat of the locomotive rose from the water and oil from the upset tender — 591,500 litres (1300 gallons) of it — flowed by in black streaks. Those who survived the crash were all rescued within a short time.

Because of the Royal tour, New Zealand's leading politicians and top officials were in Auckland, which meant that orders and administration were arranged promptly and completely once news of the disaster had been absorbed. The Prime Minister, S. G. (later Sir Sidney) Holland, was awakened at the Grand Hotel at 2 a.m. by the Commissioner of Police and he immediately went to Government House to inform the Governor-General, Sir Willoughby Norrie. He then joined a conference at the Grand Hotel attended by officers of the police, the Railways Department, the Army, broadcasting authorities and the Secretary of Internal Affairs, A. P. Harper, and a committee to supervise rescue work was set up. This was the first of four committees appointed to co-ordinate search and rescue operations, to help meet the material needs of survivors and to establish a communications network. The Auckland meeting was later joined by the Leader of the Opposition, Walter (later Sir Walter) Nash.

Prime Minister Holland left Auckland for Waiouru at 3 a.m., where a second rescue organisation was appointed after talks with Inspector W. R. Brown, the officer in charge of the Wanganui police district, who had been in charge of overnight rescue and relief work. He briefed the Prime Minister, the Prime Minister's secretary, K. M. Sleight, and the spearhead of the field group from Auckland.

Next the Prime Minister visited the Waiouru Military Camp hospital, where he first saw women survivors, all of whom were suffering from shock, bruising and cuts. They had been passengers in car Z, which had rolled over several times before landing in the swirling waters. He then visited male survivors — 'Their behaviour was magnificent and all of them were grateful to be alive.'[16]

As he told a press conference later, 'I saw the Navy, Army, Railways and MoW employees who had toiled all night and who, although almost dropping with fatigue, were still carrying on and no words of mine could hope to pay adequate tribute to them. The Navy, Army and the Police had all rendered magnificent service there.'[17]

Opposite: The grim task of seeking the dead. One of the many men who worked long hours searches the interior of a carriage.

Then followed an escorted tour over the scene of the disaster in the company of members of the Railways Commission and the General Manager of Railways, H. C. Lusty, before returning to Waiouru Camp to set up a headquarters commission to take charge of the rescue work. Through this committee, the three services would be responsible for providing clothing and other goods to those who had escaped death. The Railways Department and the Post Office, represented by the postmaster at Waiouru, would take care of financial needs. The Railways Department would transport survivors to their homes.

A press and radio committee was appointed, through which the public would be kept informed of what was happening. This committee had access to a high-powered radio transmitting set brought from Waiouru, which kept officials in direct touch with the military camp. It was also used to relay messages to various parts of New Zealand through amateur radio operators of the national Search and Rescue Organisation's emergency radio corps. Small infantry pack sets were used in the field to keep various parties in touch with the central radio base van.

Radio broadcasts from the scene of the tragedy were the only means of telling the New Zealand public what had happened, because no newspapers were published that Christmas Day, as

The Prime Minister, Mr (later Sir) Sidney Holland and the General Manager of the Railways Department, Mr H. C. Lusty, at the scene of the disaster.

is still the case. The Prime Minister spoke to New Zealand from Waiouru Military Camp early in the afternoon of Christmas Day, to give the first detailed account of the disaster.

> It is with profound regret that I have to announce that a most serious railway accident occurred to the 3 p.m. express travelling from Wellington to Auckland. The disaster occurred at 10.21 o'clock last night, three-quarters of a mile north of Tangiwai, which is 7 miles north of Waiouru.
>
> The train, which was on time at Waiouru and also at Tangiwai, reached the railway bridge crossing the Whangaehu River (sometimes called Sulphur Stream). So far as can be ascertained, a tremendous volume of water swept down the river. The cause of the tremendous and sudden flood is not known, but it apparently hit the bridge immediately before the train reached the spot.

Mr Holland went on to report what was believed to have followed and he reported on the search and rescue organisation which was operating.

> I deeply regret to say that this is the most disastrous railway accident in New Zealand's history and unfortunately it has been attended by an appalling loss of life. When the express left Taihape it carried 275 passengers. At Waiouru eight passengers left the train. Thus at the time of the disaster there were 267 passengers. Of this number, 103 have so far been accounted for and these include 56 passengers who remained in that part of the train that was not involved in the accident.
>
> Twelve persons are in the Raetihi Hospital, but I am not at the

Rescue workers shovelling silt and debris away from the mangled remains of the first carriage, A 1907, on the northern bank of the river. On the left can be seen the tender of the locomotive.

moment able to state their conditions, but will give this information when it is available. There are 21 persons in hospital at Waiouru Military Camp. These people were in the last carriage to fall into the river and all had a miraculous escape. None of these people is seriously hurt. There were 22 passengers in that carriage and all but one was rescued. Fourteen persons are being cared for by local residents in the Karioi district.

Thirteen bodies have been recovered. This leaves 151 persons unaccounted for and for whom large search parties are now operating over many miles of the river. Fifty-six of the persons accounted for returned to Marton by train and two returned to Taihape by private car.

It would be impossible to describe the scene in words. The enormous concrete piles on which the bridge rested weighed many tons and so great was the force of the flood waters these huge piers were washed far downstream. The chassis of one of the large railway carriages is now several miles downstream. Some bodies have been recovered 15 miles from the scene of the disaster. I gravely fear that there is little hope of further persons being rescued alive and it therefore appears that the death toll will be 164, of whom 13 have already been recovered.

The explanation of the difficulty in recovering bodies is that a wall of water about 20 feet high swept down the river. Enormous quantities of silt and rock have been swept downstream and it is feared that many bodies have thus been buried. Farmers and

No time was lost clearing the wreckage and driving piles for a temporary bridge at Tangiwai. This picture was taken on Boxing Day when preliminary work was well in hand for the restoration of the Main Trunk Line. In the left foreground are the crumpled remains of the locomotive, draped with rubbish from the flood.

others with properties on the bank of this river as far as the sea are asked to keep a close watch and to send reports to the nearest police station.

After reporting on the search and praising workers at the site, the Prime Minister promised that lists of names would be broadcast at the earliest possible moment. Then he concluded: 'It is with the deepest regret that I have to make this statement on Christmas Day, but I feel no doubt that it is my simple duty to do so. I know that this terrible disaster will shock all New Zealand and on behalf of the Government and myself personally I wish to express my profound sympathy with the relatives of those who have been killed or injured, or about whom there is at the moment no definite information.'[18]

For the first time a British monarch spoke from New Zealand on the evening of Christmas Day 1953 to her peoples the world over. From a room at Government House, Auckland, the Queen made her second Christmas broadcast to the Commonwealth and Empire. For New Zealand, the significant part was the last added paragraph, which became an integral part of the worldwide broadcast.

Originally the speech was to finish with a tribute to progress made by the Commonwealth in 'moving steadily towards greater harmony between its many creeds, colours and races'. To all her subjects throughout the Commonwealth she commended that Christmas hope and prayer, but the broadcast was extended to include reference to the Tangiwai disaster of the previous evening:

> And now I want to say something to my people in New Zealand. Last night a grievous railway accident took place at Tangiwai which will have brought tragedy into many homes and sorrow unto all upon this Christmas Day. I know that there is no one in New Zealand and, indeed, throughout the Commonwealth, who will not join with my husband and me in sending to those who mourn a message of sympathy in their loss. I pray that they and all who have been injured may be comforted and strengthened.[19]

Her Majesty the Queen makes her Christmas Day broadcast from Government House, Auckland.

The Queen had learnt of the disaster when the Prime Minister reported details to Government House. Later in the day Mr Holland telephoned from Waiouru with further information. Her Majesty had that morning sent to the Prime Minister a message recording her distress on learning of the 'terrible railway accident which has taken place at Tangiwai during the night'. She added: 'My husband and I share to the full the grief which will be felt by all my people, not only in New Zealand but throughout the Commonwealth and we trust that you will convey the message of our most heartfelt sympathy to the families of those who have lost their lives and to the injured.'[20] The royal message was one of hundreds which flooded into Waiouru and Wellington. Not least was that from the Governor-General, Sir Willoughby Norrie, and Lady Norrie, who mourned the loss 'of so many valuable lives'.[21]

Church services that Christmas Day were overshadowed by the tragedy. The Bishop of Auckland, the Rt. Rev. W. J. Simkin, spoke of 'the shadow of death which had overtaken this country' during the service in the cathedral church of St Mary's which the Queen and Duke of Edinburgh attended. He asked the congregation to stand in silent prayer. The Bishop of

Christchurch, the Rt. Rev. A. K. Warren, told his congregation how, while greeting the cathedral bellringers, he had found one of them had reserved a seat on that train, but had decided at the last moment to remain in Christchurch to take part in ringing the Christmas peal.

Special prayers were said at services throughout New Zealand, offering sympathy to those who had suffered loss. Mayors and other community leaders issued statements, joining their people in a tide of deep-seated feeling for the bereaved. A different note was added by the President of the Methodist Church of New Zealand, the Rev. H. L. Fiebig who, after extending sympathy on behalf of the people of his church added: 'In this unexpected natural calamity they remember also the staff of a department which renders to the community such constant and faithful service.'[22]

His remark complemented a press statement issued by the Canterbury branch of the Amalgamated Society of Railway Servants:

> Without minimising in the slightest degree national sympathy and regret for the tragic accident in the North Island, the Canterbury branch of the Amalgamated Society of Railway Servants feels that for more than 20,000 railway workers it can express the greatest sympathy to the relatives and friends of those injured and killed, because we feel, as railwaymen and railwaywomen that, although the accident was beyond our control, we are responsible for the well-being and safety of all people carried by the railway system. To the relatives and friends of those who were killed and injured we extend our greatest sympathy.[23]

News of the disaster profoundly affected the touring All Blacks' reaction to Christmas in London. At the team's Christmas dinner at their London hotel, manager J. N. Millard, proposing the one toast 'The folks at home,' said, 'We thought this would be a time of rejoicing. Instead it is one of great sadness. The disaster is constantly in our minds.'[24] The team then stood and silently honoured the toast. And they joined the crowd of nearly 20,000 at Twickenham which stood in silence for one minute in tribute to the victims. In Johannesburg the New Zealand cricket team also stood in respect before sitting down to Christmas dinner at the Wanderers' Club; one of the team's fast bowlers was to find that his fiancée was among the victims.

Sympathy messages were international. The Prime Minister of Britain, Sir Winston Churchill, joined people like Queen Elizabeth the Queen Mother, Queen Salote of Tonga, the Prime Minister of Northern Ireland, the Lord Mayor of London, Garfield Todd and the South African Prime Minister Dr Malan in expressing sorrow. Most London newspapers displayed huge pictures of the wreckage strewn in the riverbed and gave prominence to reports of the disaster. One paper said: 'Britons and New Zealanders have always been close in affection though 12,000 miles of sea divide them. Our thoughts this weekend are with those who mourn in that other island.'[25]

Prayers were said in St Paul's Cathedral, London.

While the messages of sympathy — and offers of monetary and other gifts — were being received and absorbed, repair gangs worked day and night and through rain and biting winds on the central plateau. One hundred and fifty Railways Department staff had a gap of more than 60 m to span between the stump of the old railway bridge and the northern shore over the Whangaehu River. While the new bridge of wood and steel construction was planned as a temporary structure, it would be capable of carrying the heaviest locomotives in service. The gangs worked 12 hour shifts.

No time was lost in clearing the wreckage and driving piles for a temporary bridge. This photograph taken on Boxing Day shows preliminary work well in hand. The crumpled remains of Ka 949 lie in the foreground.

Immediately after the accident, northbound buses took passengers as far as the collapsed road bridge across the Whangaehu River. There passengers crossed the river on planks to waiting buses and continued their journey. Similar arrangements applied to southbound buses. The express was diverted through Stratford, involving a 2½ hour delay, but the new bridge was open to express train traffic on New Year's Eve.

Meantime the police were bedevilled by not knowing exactly who was travelling on the train. Indeed, at first it was not known exactly how many passengers there had been and on 27 December 1953 the Prime Minister appealed to passengers who had left by private transport or other means to notify the police. The Railways Department, then as now, does not require passenger identification; all that is required is a valid ticket.

When, however, an inquiry was made by relatives who were not certain whether someone had been on the disaster train, the police listed the inquiry with the names of those concerned — it remained listed until cleared. This led to the

Minister of Defence, the Hon. T. L. MacDonald, on behalf of the Deputy Prime Minister to issue a public statement: 'It would be of material help to the Police, in their work of checking the actual train passengers, if anyone who made such an inquiry and has since ascertained that the person inquired for was not involved in the accident will inform the Police to that effect, so that those names may be deleted from the official list.'[26]

By now Tangiwai had become a place of pilgrimage. Thousands flocked to the wreck-strewn site, some to gawp, some to weep. Most watched silently as cameras clicked beside the rusting wheels of carriages. Wreckage lay over a wide area,

Only six days after the Tangiwai disaster trains were again crossing the Whangaehu River. The Wellington to Auckland daylight limited express is crossing the temporary bridge, after the Main Trunk Line was reopened.

with the riverbanks torn by the Christmas Eve torrent, by machinery and by many footprints. At night a patrol covered the temporary bridge in the glare of floodlights. Trains moved over it dead slow. Souvenir hunters scrambled through the wreckage. Small fittings disappeared (when they could be found) and the ground was littered with the wrappings from rolls of unexposed film. A few tattered clothes still lay blackened by oil and torn by the current, even at the end of the first week of the new year.

Downsteam the search for bodies continued. Search parties used packhorses, tractors and sledges to recover victims. Hampered by rain and a sometimes flooded river, searchers nevertheless continued to find bodies along the riverbanks. By 27 December, three days after the tragedy, search parties had four times covered the 130 km (80 mile) stretch from the wrecked bridge to the sea. High precipitous banks had added to the difficulties and in some places only experienced bushmen had been able to search. Many farmers went looking themselves, recovering bodies and taking them to the nearest road to be ferried to Waiouru by Army transport. Ropes were necessary at one point 22 km (14 miles) below the bridge to lower men down a cliff-face before four bodies were recovered.

Several hundred people were engaged in the search, drawn, it seemed, from everywhere — Legion of Frontiersmen, the Search and Rescue Organisation, civilian volunteers from many parts of the North Island, even as far away as Matamata and Te Awamutu. 'Throughout there is a good spirit, a will to help and no thought of stopping in the long search hours from dawn to darkness,' said a Press Association message filed from Waiouru on 27 December. A major search for bodies was made on 3 January when more than 300 people were organised to work from the mouth of the Whangaehu River to the scene of the accident. Piles of weed and debris were broken up in the quest.

Generally the search parties were made up of 10 men, five on each side of the river. The length of river allotted to each party was small, so that a thorough search could be made. Boats were used in sections of the river and axes and cross-cut saws broke up piles of debris. Each party had a walkie-talkie radio, enabling members to direct search operations on the opposite side of the river; this saved a tremendous amount of walking.

Of all the bodies recovered, 60 were found 24 km (15 miles) from the accident scene. Twenty people were never accounted for and only 28 of the second-class passengers on the train survived.

When the crest of the flood in the Whangaehu River arrived near Wanganui on Friday afternoon, the day after Christmas Day, it carried so much debris that an experienced boatman refused to go out on it. A churning mass of pillows, books, suitcases and woodwork from the wrecked trains was swept down river about 160 km (100 miles) from the scene of the disaster. It was the same river which carried some bodies out to sea. A rope barrier strung across the river at at Whangaehu, about 10 km (6 miles) from the mouth, was probably too late to recover some bodies. Searchlights were trained on the barrier at night.

Coroners' courts were held continuously with local justices of the peace taking sworn statements of identification from relatives. For many the waiting was the worst and, as the dead were brought in, the sad, quiet groups would come hopefully forward. Police did all they could to ease the suffering of these mothers and fathers, wives and husbands. There was religious comfort, too, from the padres, priests, Protestant clergymen and Salvation Army workers, all of whom came as quickly as they could. They helped many who had been stunned and shocked by the suddenness of the tragedy.

On Sunday 27 December, four nights after the disaster, a special train of railway wagons with huge white crosses chalked on their sides pulled out of Waiouru, carrying the dead home for burial. A total of 114 bodies had been recovered and it was thought 37 people were still missing. The train also carried unidentified bodies to Wellington and from then on

The wrecked and twisted road bridge across the Whangaehu River. Temporary erected wooden beams gave fast access between the north and south banks in the days following the disaster.

Mount Ruapehu in 1954, seen from the Bailey bridge which temporarily replaced the wrecked highway bridge. The only remaining evidence of the disaster is the massive concrete pier lying on its side in mid river between the two restored bridges.

relatives would seek to identify next of kin at the Wellington Public Hospital.

An emergency committee had its first meeting in Wellington that same day under the chairmanship of K. J. (later Sir Keith) Holyoake, the Deputy Prime Minister, and set to work on similar lines to that of the committee at Waiouru. Its members included the Leader of the Opposition, the Hon. Walter Nash, and representatives of the police, the Army, the Railways Department, the Wellington Hospital Board plus financial directors. The Minister of Defence, the Hon. T. L. MacDonald, took over responsibility from the Prime Minister at Waiouru and Mr Holland returned to Auckland.

A public memorial service for victims of the disaster was held in Westminster Abbey on Friday 8 January 1954. Next of kin of British victims were specially invited to this service. Lord Freyberg, VC, represented the Queen, the Very Rev. A. C. Don, Dean of Westminster, conducted the service, and the Rt. Rev. G. V. Gerard, Assistant Bishop of Sheffield and former Bishop of Waiapu, gave the address. The lesson was read by the High Commissioner for New Zealand, Sir Frederick Doidge. The north and south transepts of the Abbey were packed by some 1400 New Zealanders, and friends and relatives of those who had lost their lives at Tangiwai. In the choir stalls were the Lord Mayor of London, prominent New Zealanders and English people closely associated with New Zealand.

On the last day of 1953, 21 unknown victims were laid to rest in the Karori Lawn Cemetery in Wellington. The 21 coffins were placed side by side in an 18 m (60 ft) grave. On top of each was a small posy. Ponga ferns were laid around the sides of the graves and on these were placed a hundred or more wreaths from all over New Zealand. There was one from the New Settlers' Association, of Wellington, 'In memory of the immigrants who died at Tangiwai.' Another, anonymous, had the brief inscription, 'To somebody's loved ones.' The Duke of Edinburgh and Prime Minister Holland, both of whom flew from Hamilton for the service, were at the graveside.

The service was begun by the chairman of the New Zealand Inter-Church Council on Foreign Affairs, the Rev. G. H. Goodman. The scripture lesson from the Book of Revelations,

At the graveside during the mass burial of unidentified victims of the Tangiwai rail disaster. The lesson is being read by Lieutenant Commissioner Hoggard, of the Salvation Army. Behind him stand the then Primate, Archbishop Owen, and the Duke of Edinburgh.

Chapter XXI, verses i–xii, was read by Lieutenant Commissioner R. A. Hoggard, Salvation Army territorial commander. The Catholic part of the service was taken by the Coadjutor Archbishop of New Zealand, the Most Rev. P. McKeefrey, and the brief address was given by the Primate of New Zealand, the Most Rev. R. H. Owen.

Our Christian faith, he said, gave comfort and solace to the mourning. 'Nothing could remove the heartache of separation, but faith in God. God knew that human sufferings were too hard to bear alone. So He sent His son to help and heal and save. Disasters like this which overshadow the country make us realise we are in the midst of death, but the triumphant assurances of Christ take us through death into life with God. While we offer to the bereaved the deepest sympathy of their fellow countrymen, which has been nobly expressed by Her Majesty the Queen and shown by the journey here and presence of the Duke of Edinburgh and the Prime Minister, we would ask you to face your sorrow with faith and a brave heart, for your dear ones are in the keeping of the Lord.'[27]

At the end of the service the Duke of Edinburgh gently placed a chaplet-shaped wreath of predominantly blue flowers near the head of the grave. The wreath bore the inscription,

The Duke of Edinburgh speaking to mourning relatives and friends at the burial service for unidentified victims at the Karori Lawn Cemetery, Wellington.

'From Elizabeth R. and the Duke of Edinburgh.' The Duke then moved across to the mourning relatives and friends to speak briefly with each of them. For nearly 10 minutes he stayed among them. Unexpected as it was, many found this the most moving part of the funeral and it was a joy to see the sudden lighting up of sad expressions. His Royal Highness spent only a short time with each, but it was surely a moment in their grief they would never forget. On the return flight to Hamilton the Royal aircraft, at the Duke's request, flew over the scene of the disaster at Tangiwai and over the crater of Mount Ruapehu.

A memorial at the head of the mass grave at the Karori Cemetery was unveiled at a service in March 1957. The names of all known to have perished are inscribed on a tablet there. Some identified since the 1953 burial service, had been removed for private internment.

Guard of the train, Mr W. I. Inglis, wearing his British Empire Medal after the investiture. Mr Inglis was a principal witness both at the coroner's inquest and the board of inquiry.

On the last day of the Royal tour of New Zealand, the Queen honoured the four heroes of the disaster. Cyril Ellis and John Holman both received the George Medal for their acts of bravery in saving 21 people trapped in the sixth carriage. The guard, William Ian Inglis, was decorated with the British Empire Medal, for the great courage and coolness he displayed in ensuring there was no passenger panic. Arthur Dewar Bell also received the British Empire Medal for the great initiative and courage he showed in being responsible for the rescue of some 15 people.

John Holman was on holiday in the Marlborough Sounds when he read of his award in the evening newspaper. 'By God, dear,' he told his wife, 'I have won the George Medal.'[28] The Post Office had telephoned some 70 accommodation houses, launch drivers and cottages in the hope of finding him, without success. Only four New Zealanders had received the George Medal, in New Zealand, before the Tangiwai awards were made.

Tangiwai survivors, Mr and Mrs J. C. Falloon and their daughter Glenis wave goodbye to the Queen and the Duke of Edinburgh, who called on this family staying with relatives at One Tree Hill, Auckland.

One other Royal recognition was a visit made by the Queen and Duke to survivors staying with friends at One Tree Hill. They were Mr and Mrs J. C. Falloon, of Christchurch, and their 16-year-old daughter, Glenis, who had been passengers in the last carriage to fall into the river. There was no formality about this meeting in the pleasant sitting room of the suburban home of Mrs Falloon's sister. The Queen said she had wished to see, in their own home, some who had been in the train crash and to express her sympathy personally.

The memorial to all who died at Tangiwai is unveiled in March 1957. Wreaths cover the graves of 16 of the victims.

Relatives and friends of victims of the disaster at Tangiwai read the names inscribed on the memorial tablet after the unveiling of the memorial in the Karori Lawn Cemetery, Wellington.

Judge W. F. Stilwell,

Professor H. J. Hopkins

Sir William Appleton.

BOARD OF INQUIRY

The board of inquiry into the Tangiwai railway disaster sat in Wellington between 26 January and 2 April 1954. Fifty-eight witnesses were heard and 74 exhibits were handed in. Evidence given before the board filled five volumes totalling 1360 pages.

Judge W. F. Stilwell was chairman of the board and its two members were Professor H. J. Hopkins, professor of Civil Engineering at Canterbury University College and Sir William Appleton, a former Mayor of Wellington. Judge Stilwell had been appointed to the bench of the Arbitration Court in 1949 and had considerable experience as chairman of various Government tribunals, including the Government Railways Industrial Tribunal (1944–62). He held the rank of lieutenant colonel on the Reserve of Officers and had a Military Cross. Mr R. Hardie Boys (later Mr Justice Hardie Boys) appeared as counsel assisting the board. The secretary was Mr J. D. Murray.

Mr Ian Macarthur appeared as counsel appointed by the Government to watch over the interests of relatives and friends of those who had lost their lives. Other counsel were Mr N. R. Bain (Wanganui) with Mr R. A. Burns (Wellington) for the Railways Department; Mr H. R. C. Wild who later, as Chief Justice, became Sir Richard Wild and Mr E. D. Blundell (later Sir Denis Blundell, Governor-General), for the relatives of the engine driver and fireman of the train, and the Engine Drivers', Firemen's and Cleaners' Association and Amalgamated Society of Railway Servants; Mr S. G. Stephenson, for the Professional Engineers' Association. Mr A. R. Tarr, General Secretary of the New Zealand Railway Officers' Institute, also appeared officially.

The order of reference set by the Minister of Railways, the Hon. W. S. Goosman, was to inquire into the following:

> What was the cause of the accident.
>
> Whether at any material time or times any person in the service of the New Zealand Government failed to exercise reasonable care or to fulfil any duty or responsibility reasonably to be expected of him in relation to the circumstances leading to the accident.
>
> Generally to inquire into and report upon such other matters arising out of the accident as may come to its notice in the course of its inquiries and which it considers should be investigated, and upon any matters affecting the premises which it considers should be brought to the Minister's attention.
>
> What steps (if any) should be taken to prevent a similar accident.

Relating what he referred to as the 'bare facts', Mr Hardie Boys said the express left Waiouru station at 10.09 p.m. There were two postal officials travelling in the postal van at the rear of the train and 268 passengers on board, according to a tally taken after leaving Waiouru. But in light of established figures of people missing and believed to have been on board the train, the total was 10 more than that. One hundred and thirty were known to be dead and it was reckoned 21 others, now missing, also perished.

Mr Hardie Boys pointed out that 'From Tangiwai Station to Karioi, the next station north, the railway line runs for a substantial distance in a dead straight line on a slightly rising grade of about one in 20.'

S. C. Manhire, a carpenter, gave evidence about an earth tremor he felt at Waiouru Army housing settlement at 7.50 p.m. on the night of the accident. Then, just on 8.30 p.m. he had heard a roaring noise, not unduly loud, but by 9 p.m. it had increased to 'a terrific roar'. Constable L. S. Smidt, of Waiouru, confirmed this unusual noise which, he said, came in waves.

Warrant Officer T. W. Pawson, of Waiouru Military Camp, who was driving from Ohakune to Waiouru, said the express seemed to be slowing down as it approached the bridge. His impression was that the engine and the carriage immediately behind it had almost cleared the bridge when the engine headlight beam shone upward momentarily. He saw two lighted carriages drop and disappear.

Robert Sommerville, a Post and Telegraph Department employee at Ohakune, told of arriving in his car on the northern side of the road bridge. His strong torch, he said, would not penetrate the smoke which was in the air. When the smoke cleared he and a companion saw a man thigh-deep in water about 50 yds (45 m) away. Between them the water was turbulent and he saw one or two large boulders being swept down the river. Later the witness came across about six injured people, covered in oil and silt.

Clifton Barltrop, of Taumarunui, watched from the road as the train neared the rail bridge. 'As the train approached, I saw a torch light on the line being flashed on and off. The train seemed to slow down when approaching the bridge.'[1] Asked by the chairman, Judge Stilwell, if he thought this slowing up was due to the waving of the torch, Barltrop said that was the impression he formed.

The guard of the train, W. I. Inglis, who received the British Empire Medal for bravery in rescue work after the accident, knew engine driver Charles Parker, who died in the accident, to be a 'top-rate driver'. Inglis had no idea how far the train was from the bridge when the emergency brakes were applied, but it would not have been very far. Re-examined by Mr Hardie Boys, the guard said he had noticed nothing to indicate whether the application of the brakes was a human factor or whether it had resulted from the breaking of a hose, but he thought the driver had applied them.

Inglis described the scene in Z car, the last car to fall into the water, which he boarded just before it toppled over. There had been no undue panic, although a few people had screamed when the carriage began to rock and bounce violently, before it tipped on its side to the left. Men walked towards the car from the riverbank in water about knee-deep to form a human chain

Mr Justice Hardie Boys.

Sir Denis Blundell.

Sir Richard Wild.

and take passengers off the car.

A man who entered Z car from a rear carriage after the train stopped, E. J. Hartnell, of Wanganui, praised the conduct of the guard, whose advice to passengers to get out of the carriage enabled them to be rescued. 'If they had been caught unawares in their seats the passengers on the right side of the car would have been thrown on top of the others,' he said. 'Those on the left would then have been under water and their chance of survival would have been less.'[2]

Engine driver D. Bentley took a mixed train across the Whangaehu River bridge about 7.25 p.m. on Christmas Eve. It was still daylight and there was only the normal amount of water in the river at that time. Later, after hearing of the disaster, he ran a special breakdown train to the north end of the bridge. Inspecting what remained of the controls on the boiler of the locomotive he noted that the oil control valve had been shut off. It must have been closed by the fireman before the disaster. It would have put the fire out, so some danger must have been apparent to the fireman for him to have shut off the valve. The damage was too great for Bentley to assess what measures had been taken by the engine driver. If a waving torch had been seen on the line ahead, the train would have been brought to a stop. If the torch were a little to the side of the track the witness agreed the driver might pause before stopping.

Mr Blundell asked Bentley at what speed he would take the express across the bridge and he replied at not more than 40 miles (65 km) an hour if the train were on time. Any unusual signal would be treated as an indication of danger. A torch light a quarter of a mile (400 m) away and outside the beam of the headlight would be picked up distinctly. Bentley said he had all the confidence in the world in the bridge — 'It never frightened me,' he said. He agreed Mr Parker had a reputation for being a careful driver and the fireman was regarded as the most efficient in the depot.[3]

Inspector W. J. K. Brown, in charge of the Wanganui police district, told the inquiry of police organisation at the scene of the tragedy. He had alerted hospitals throughout the area when news of the accident was received at 11.15 p.m. He had ordered all police in his district to the scene and called for assistance from other districts. On Christmas Day, he appealed to farmers and other residents to keep a watch for bodies on the river.

He told how bodies retrieved from the river were silt-covered and some were coated in thick oil from the locomotive. The bodies were washed and laid out 'as decently as possible'.[4] With large crowds assembled at Waiouru to help identification, inquests were held night and day. The police, Brown said, 'carried out their duties in a most creditable manner and worked long hours with little sleep to handle this dreadful calamity.'[5]

The inspector said that if there were ever another disaster on the scale of Tangiwai it would be in everyone's interests to

Tremendous deposits of silt half buried some of the wreckage in the riverbed. Here a bogie is partly visible beneath the wreckage of car Z.

have a representative of the undertakers on the scene early; there had been initial difficulties in arranging with undertakers for the supply of coffins.

The chairman asked, 'Could you indicate whether throughout New Zealand there is an organisation within the Police Department to deal with catastrophes or emergencies associated with them?'[6] Brown's reply was: 'No. The reliance is mainly on the officer in charge of the district.'[7]

George Medal winner Cyril Ellis, of Taihape, was in Australia when the inquiry began and returned to appear before the board later in its hearings. He repeated his graphic story: 'I more or less prayed to God that it would get through. Seconds later the engine just disappeared, together with the first carriage, with a thunderous roar.'[8]

George Medal winner, Mr A. C. Ellis, holding the five-cell torch with which he tried in vain to stop the express before it reached the Tangiwai bridge.

As he turned round after waving at the train with his torch he saw that the railway bridge was intact. He could see only the top part of the line itself, which was definitely intact.

Mr Hardie Boys: 'Would you, do you think, have noticed it if the pier had been gone?'

Witness: 'I doubt it very much.'

Mr Hardie Boys: 'Do you reckon that if there had been a gap in the rails you would have noticed it in that line of light along the bridge?'

Witness: 'Definitely'.[9]

Expert evidence calculated that a train travelling at 38 miles (60 km) an hour would have taken approximately six seconds from where Mr Ellis was standing for the engine to plunge into the rivers. Cyril Ellis told Mr N. R. Bain, for the Railways Department, that he saw both rails on the bridge when the engine passed him.

SOURCE OF THE FLOOD

Of witnesses who gave evidence on the source of the water which roared down the Whangaehu River on Christmas Eve, two in particular led the field.

R. Sheffield, of Gisborne, chief guide at the Chateau Tongariro about 20 years before, appeared before the board on 4

Members of a climbing party making a first inspection of the upper collapse hole in the ice of the Whangaehu Glacier. Inspection confirmed that the discharge from the Crater Lake was through an ice cave rather than by eruptive force over the low lip of the crater.

March 1954. He considered that all the water which went into the river had come from the crater lake on Mount Ruapehu. It all flowed, and was still flowing, from under the foot of the Whangaehu Glacier at the place which was the normal source of the Whangaehu River. At the crater there was now an area of lake floor about one-fifth of the total lake area exposed and it was clear that the lake level had fallen some 20–25 ft (6–7 m).

On 14 January last Sheffield had swum in the lake, as he had done on several occasions, and the temperature seemed the same around the edge, about 74°F (24°C). In the wall of the lake he had found a large cave shaped like a concert soundshell, some 30 ft (9 m) high, 50 ft (15 m) wide and about 50 ft (15 m) deep to where the roof and floor met. While he was at the lake there were three falls of ice, two outside the cave entrance and one inside.

'In 1936–37, when I was chief guide at the Chateau, I entered the ice tunnel where the present cave now is by swimming into it under water,' Sheffield said. 'The tunnel opened up inside to give head room and I went in 60 ft (18 m) to the limit of my rope.' Water was flowing through the tunnel in the direction of the Whangaehu Glacier. He entered the present cave on this year's visit and spent about five minutes examining the interior. 'Then part of the roof collapsed alongside me and discouraged further investigation,' he added.[10]

The roof of the cave was made of large slabs of ice, cracked and ready to peel off. The floor was covered with broken ice from the roof. At the back of the cave a small amount of water was flowing through an opening about 4 ft (1.2 m) wide and 1 ft (30 cm) high and in the direction of the glacier.

On 25 January Sheffield said he followed the Whangaehu River up to its source at the foot of the Whangaehu Glacier. The river did not disappear for any part of its length and its flow was confined to one channel and was normal. He had sampled the water at various points and it was always sulphurous, very strongly so at its source at the foot of the glacier, as strong as the lake itself. There was nothing at all to indicate that the floodwaters came from anywhere but the crater lake, through the normal source of the Whangaehu River at the foot of the glacier.

GEOLOGIST'S EVIDENCE

Mr James Healy, of the Government Geological Survey, with a model of Mount Ruapehu which he produced in support of his testimony at the board of inquiry.

The superintending geologist of the Government Geological Survey, James Healy, on 9 March told the inquiry he believed an ash barrier on the edge of Mount Ruapehu's crater lake had collapsed suddenly about 8 p.m. on Christmas Eve, precipitating a solid mass of water down the channel to the Whangaehu River. Healy said his investigations had produced no evidence that volcanic activity had played any part in causing the collapse of the barriers, but this could not be definitely ruled out.

Evidence gathered from the scene of the train crash indicated that the two central piers of the bridge had collapsed before the train reached the bridge. In his opinion the flood or lahar (a mudflow occurring in volcanic areas) had sufficient density and velocity to carry these central piers forward bodily.

The presence of an ice cave on Ruapehu, leading to the Whangaehu River, had been known for some time. After the accident the roof of this small cave could be seen above a pile of fallen ice at the front of a large cave, which had been formed apparently by the collapse of volcanic rock. This cave was about 150 feet (45 m) wide and 100 feet (30 m) high at the entrance, although its size diminished rapidly inside. By 29 December the lake level had fallen about 27 ft (8 m).

'While the lake was discharging through the first formed cave, water must have also been seeping through the volcanic ash and scoria alongside to form another channel beneath the ice at a lower level,' said Healy. 'Erosion in this channel may have reduced the strength of the ash barrier and cracking movements in the ice above may have caused it to collapse suddenly.'[11]

The seismograph at the Chateau, while not recording any earthquake or volcanic disturbance, did record vibration, probably caused by the rush of water beginning two or three minutes after 8 p.m. on 24 December.

An ice bridge which had been observed in the Whangaehu

Inside the Crater Lake showing the ice cave through which the floodwater surged at the far end. Adjacent to the main cave is a smaller cave (left), its mouth almost buried with rubble. The former lake level was 7.5 m (25 ft) higher.

Close-up aerial view of the larger cave, taken on 28 December. The smaller cave partly blocked by rubble is also to be seen. Some slightly crevassed ice appears to the right of the main cave. Aerial inspection showed the crater lip to be a lava sheet overlain by ash and scoria to varying depths, all solidly ice-bound.

Glacier was presumably thin, Healy continued, and when the mass of water from the crater lake surged down the channel, either the vibrations and pressure cracked and shattered the ice, or a temporary blockage beneath the ice caused the pressure to mount until the ice gave way. Huge masses of broken ice must have been carried away by the flood.

Healy said the flood or lahar reached Tangiwai about 10.10 or 10.15 p.m. in the form of a dense wave of water, sand and boulders, removing two piers which brought down three girders. When the train arrived at 10.21 p.m. the engine apparently crashed into a third pier and a fourth was also broken. One of the central 44 ft (13 m) girders was found downstream from the bridge on the right bank, embedded in the sand deposit and full of sand and boulders up to 4 ft (1.25 m) in diameter, indicating it was washed down in the early stages of the lahar. The first carriage and tender had come to rest

Looking upstream from the railway embankment on the left bank of the Whangaehu River, with the deposit of boulders and sand left by the flood in the foreground. In the left background is the well-defined level of the sand terrace on the right bank. On the extreme right is the surface of the sand terrace on the left bank, dotted with rounded boulders of vesicular andesite.

immediately upstream of the girder and at a higher level.

'This evidence indicates,' Healy said, 'that the two central piers were carried away bodily in the first stage of the lahar.' He considered that the lahar would have had a transporting ability many times that of a normal river in flood. He added: 'It is suggested that this supports the argument for believing that two piers [went] in the first stage of the lahar.'[12]

The train, in his opinion, had reached the bridge while the lahar was at its peak, but shortly afterwards the wave had receded and erosion began. Most of the sand was washed away, leaving sand terraces along the banks. The lahar had taken about 10–15 minutes to pass, after which the river level had fallen rapidly; by next morning the river had almost returned to its normal flow but was still carrying silt.

Healy said that from the crater lake 70 million ft^3 (476,000 m^3) of water had escaped down the Whangaehu River about the time of the disaster. About one-sixth of this — nearly 12 million ft^3 (336,000 m^3) — came down to make headwaters of the flood. The remainder drained in gradually diminishing quantity immediately after.

Lahars (turbulent mudflows associated with volcanic activity) had swept down the Whangaehu River five times in the previous 93 years — in 1861, 1889, 1895, 1925 and 1953. 'The floods of 1861, 1925 and 1953 appeared to have been cold lahars, due to the release of lake water below the glacier,' Healy said 'Those of 1889 and 1895 resulted from eruptions in the crater lake. The flooding appears to have been considerable on at least four occasions.'[13]

Healy told Mr E. D. Blundell that Ruapehu was 'by no means extinct.' When Mr Blundell asked whether there was always the possibility of a sudden discharge of water from the lake into the Whangaehu, the geologist replied, 'There is a possibility that the water can be discharged, say over the rim or as a result of volcanic activity. That position was watched at the beginning of the 1945 eruption.'

Healy told Mr A. R. Tarr, representing the Railway Officers' Institute, that his department had not kept a regular watch on the level of water in the crater lake. Before the disaster he personally had not felt apprehensive about travelling by train in the National Park area, and he thought that no one else should have had cause for anxiety.

Looking downstream from where the express plunged off the bridge. Wrecked carriages crushed like broken sardine tins lie tossed on each side of the river by the receding floodwaters.

ENGINEERING EVIDENCE

Railways Department District Mechanical Engineer at Auckland, W. R. Butcher, thought the brakes of the Tangiwai express had been applied 700 ft (200 m) from the bridge. After the accident, the locomotive had been found to be in foregear, as would be consistent if the brakes had been applied before the crash.

Butcher gave the inquiry his considered opinion as to how the express fell from the bridge and outlined the damage sustained by the rolling stock. Evidently the bridge girders had sagged as the locomotive ran on to the track and the train ran down this drooping track and struck the north pier of the bridge, rolled to the left and fell into the river. In the fall the tender had probably been wrenched off, with part of the locomotive frame, and, because of its construction, was swept downstream and stranded on the northern bank approximately 50 yds (45 m) from the locomotive.

'I assume that the leading car on the train, A 1907, rode above the tender as the tender fell and that the leading end of the underframe of this car struck the first shore pier on the north side and was bent upward.'

Butcher's examination of the locomotive and cars had revealed the following damage:

Locomotive Ka 949: Leading bogie torn off. It was subsequently recovered a few yards away from the leading end of the boiler.

Leading heatstock bent and driven back, buckling the main engine frame plates ahead of the cylinders and wrecking the front drawbar dragbox. Smokebox crushed in and front plate forced back. Air brake pumps broken off. Trailing driving wheels of locomotive broken. Portions of the wheel centres, spokes and tyres were broken out. Cab torn away from the footplate and boiler. The cab had been extensively crushed. Cab fittings wrenched off. An examination of the top header regulator on the locomotive, in the smokebox, showed that the valves admitting steam to the steam chest were closed, evidently by the engine-driver. The back plate of the tender was practically unmarked and it was evident that car A 1907 did not run into the back of the tender. The tender tank sustained only superficial damage, but both bogies were torn off.

Locomotive Ka 949 in happier days.

The wrecked locomotive was taken to pieces for removal from the riverbank. Otherwise it would have been too heavy to move.

The buckled end shows the force with which the first carriage presumably hit a bridge pier. Between it and the overturned locomotive tender (right) is all that remained of the locomotive cab.

Carriage A 1907, 2nd class, No. 1 on train, Car E

This car was approximately 80 yards (70 m) downstream from the bridge on the northern bank of the river. Approximately 10 feet (3 m) of the leading end of the car underframe was bent vertically, almost at right angles to the floor.

This portion of the car body was destroyed. A portion of the anti-collision end, although crumpled and damaged, was still attached to the underframe. It had obviously taken a heavy shock. The remainder of the car body was superficially damaged and the underframe was twisted. Both bogies had been displaced but were recovered, one near the locomotive and one beneath the car.

Carriage A 1899, 2nd class, No. 2 on train, Car D

This car evidently fell directly into the gap behind car 1907 and was completely wrecked and stripped of its body in a very short distance. The car was in the river almost opposite car A 1907 and approximately 80 (70 m) yards from the railway bridge. The whole of the car body was missing, only the twisted underframe and seat frame wreckage remaining. Both bogies were still attached by brake rods to the underframe.

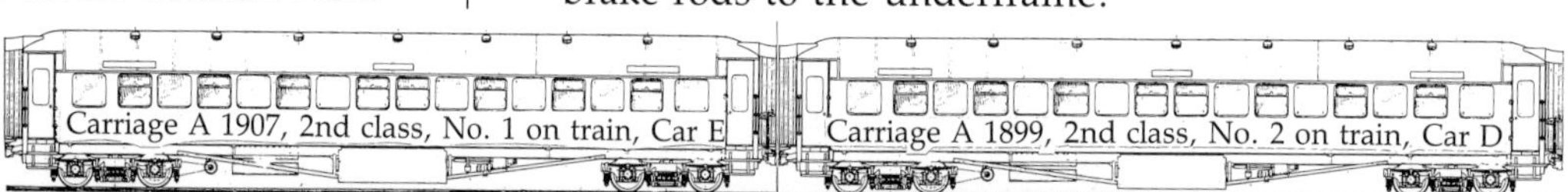

Overturned wreckage of the second carriage, stripped of its body and lying 73 m (80 yds) downstream from the railway bridge. In the background the first carriage rests on the northern bank.

Little was left of the third carriage, seen lying beside a demolished span of the bridge, with the ill-fated locomotive lying on its side beyond.

Carriage A 1915, 2nd class, No. 3 on train, Car C
When this car fell into the gap, it is evident that a displaced girder still hanging from the north end finally fell with and trapped this car, demolishing approximately half the car body. This car had come to rest upstream of the locomotive alongside a bridge girder on the northern bank. Half of the car body was totally destroyed down to floor level. The remainder of the car body and the underframe were wrecked during the search for victims. One bogie off this car was recovered from the silt around the car. The other bogie was never recovered.

Carriage A 1862, 2nd class, No. 4 on train, Car B
I cannot account for this car being swept past the road bridge. This car was stranded high on the northern bank approximately 160 yards (145 metres) downstream from the railway bridge. The underframe was badly twisted and damaged. The car roof and sides down to window ledge were missing. The seat frames and lower sides of the car body were wrecked. One vestibule end frame was intact but damaged. One bogie was still connected to the underframe by the brake pull rod and it was on top of the car floor.

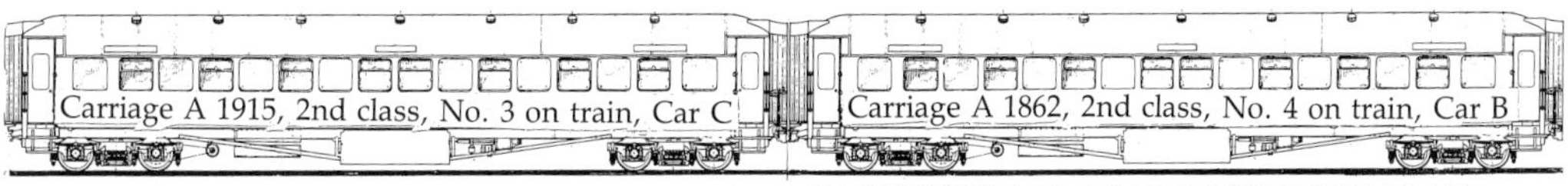

The fourth carriage was reduced to this skeleton of twisted steel. One of the bogies came to rest on top of the seats.

The remains of carriage A 1920, the fifth on the train, were found some 2.5 km (1½ miles) downstream from the railway bridge.

Carriage A 1920, 2nd class, No. 5 on train, Car A

This car had passed the road bridge and was found stranded on a shoal mid-river approximately 1½ miles (2½ km) downstream from the railway bridge. The whole of the car body above floor level was missing. One bogie was still attached to and under the car. Both this car and the fourth car, A 1862, must have fallen into the gap at the height of the flood.

Carriage Aa 1717, 1st class, No. 6 on train, Car Z

When the girder on which this car was standing, fell, the flood must have subsided considerably as it was swept only a short distance, being stranded on its side high on the southern bank approximately 60 yards (55 metres) downstream from the bridge. It came to rest, canted — approximately 15 degrees. The lower or south side was embedded in silt almost up to window ledge level. When righting the car with a bulldozer to facilitate the search for victims, the car body was cut by ropes and the underframe twisted. Both bogies were under this car.[14]

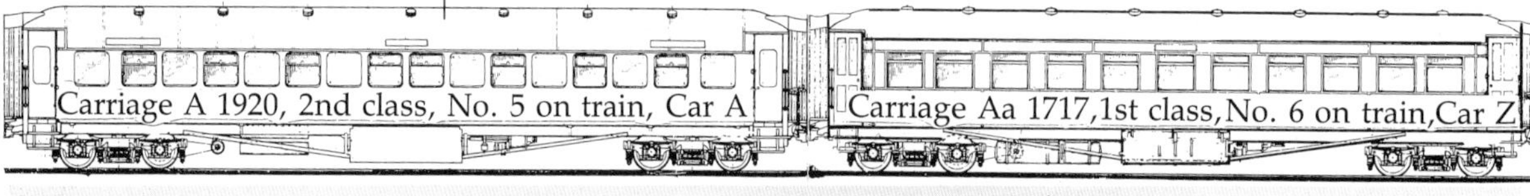

In the foreground are the crumpled remains of the second carriage, A 1899. On the left is part of the bridge's massive central pier, which was swept away like straw. In the background is car Z.

Part of the third carriage being hauled from the riverbed. The other half lay alongside the locomotive on the opposite riverbank.

Carriage A 1887, 1st class, No. 7 on train, Car X
This car was *not* derailed. The vestibule end fabric concertina was ripped off back to the car end.[15]

Cars left on the line were: First-class carriages A 1857, car V; and A 1889, car W; brake van F 592 and postal van Fp 707.

To Mr Ian Macarthur, counsel watching over the interests of relatives and friends of those who had lost their lives, Butcher said he thought the brake on the expresses services 'as good as it is possible to obtain and the maintenance of the brake on those trains is kept up to a very high standard.'

Mr Macarthur: '. . . to those of us who are not greatly experienced in braking systems, it does seem, at first sight, that a distance of some 700 ft (210 m) or thereabouts is a long way for a train to run before the brakes can bring the train to a standstill.'

Witness: 'I will agree that on paper it does seem a long distance, but in the field it does not seem so very long when we are working on a question of miles and not of yards.'[16]

To Mr E. D. Blundell, Butcher described a test he had made a fortnight before to determine what an engine driver could see at night with the lights on a straight stretch: 'I made a test . . . at Frankton on a train without any prearranging. We stopped at 2 miles (3 km) south of Frankton in the swamp. I asked the engine driver to pop the whistle when I was going out of his sight in the centre of the track. We pegged out that distance and the maximum width and I measured it off the following morning and I found that I was 10 chains (200 m) from the front end of the locomotive when the driver said I was going out of sight . . . That was a check made on a locomotive without any prearrangement or adjustment or cleaning of the reflector and I should say that the headlight, the normal headlight, would be fully effective at 300 yds (275 m).'[17]

APPLICATION OF BRAKES

Acting Chief Mechanical Engineer of the Railways Department, C. T. Bishop, told the inquiry he believed the driver of the train had applied the emergency brakes 700 ft (200 m) from the bridge. Had the brakes not been applied at that distance, more or even all the carriages would have fallen into the river.

With an initial speed of 50 miles (80 km) an hour, which was assumed to be the speed at which the train had been travelling, the brakes had to be applied 1177 ft (350 m) back for the train to stop just clear of the break. From 40 miles (65 km) an hour, the stopping distance was 777 ft (230 m).[18]

The Acting Chief Mechanical Engineer of the Railways Department, H. Z. Purchase, said he had calculated that the speed of the locomotive as it came on to the bridge was about 38 miles (60 km) an hour. 'If travelling at 50 miles an hour the engine driver would have to receive warning when about 750 ft (225 m) from the bridge for an emergency application to be made which would stop the foremost of the rear three cars at the end of the remaining rails.'

Purchase considered the position of the valve motion gear and the driving wheels on the locomotive indicated that the driver had been aware of trouble ahead and had either shut off steam or left the steam valve closed. That a number of carriages stopped on the southern side of the bridge without excessive jolting indicated that the brakes had been applied 'at some time when the locomotive was between the bridge and a point 750 ft (225 m) south of the bridge.'[19]

Routine inspections of the Tangiwai railway bridge had not recorded anything unusual about the bridge or the state of the river, said H. G. Stevens, a Railways ways and works engineer stationed at Wanganui. He acknowledged that the source of a mysterious flood in the Whangaehu River in 1925 had never been investigated. Evidence had shown that after the 1925 flood a pier supporting the Tangiwai railway bridge had tilted half an inch (12 mm) and the track above had bulged to the same extent. 'It is,' said Stevens, 'perhaps unfortunate that this occurrence was not investigated but the scour was not a serious one.'[20]

During the month before the 1953 Tangiwai disaster the Inspector of Permanent Way at Ohakune, F. W. Beccard, had carried out the following inspections of the bridge:

1. By motor trolley on 26 November 1953, 3 December 1953 and 16 December 1953.
2. Walked the length and inspected it in company with the ganger on 17 November 1953.

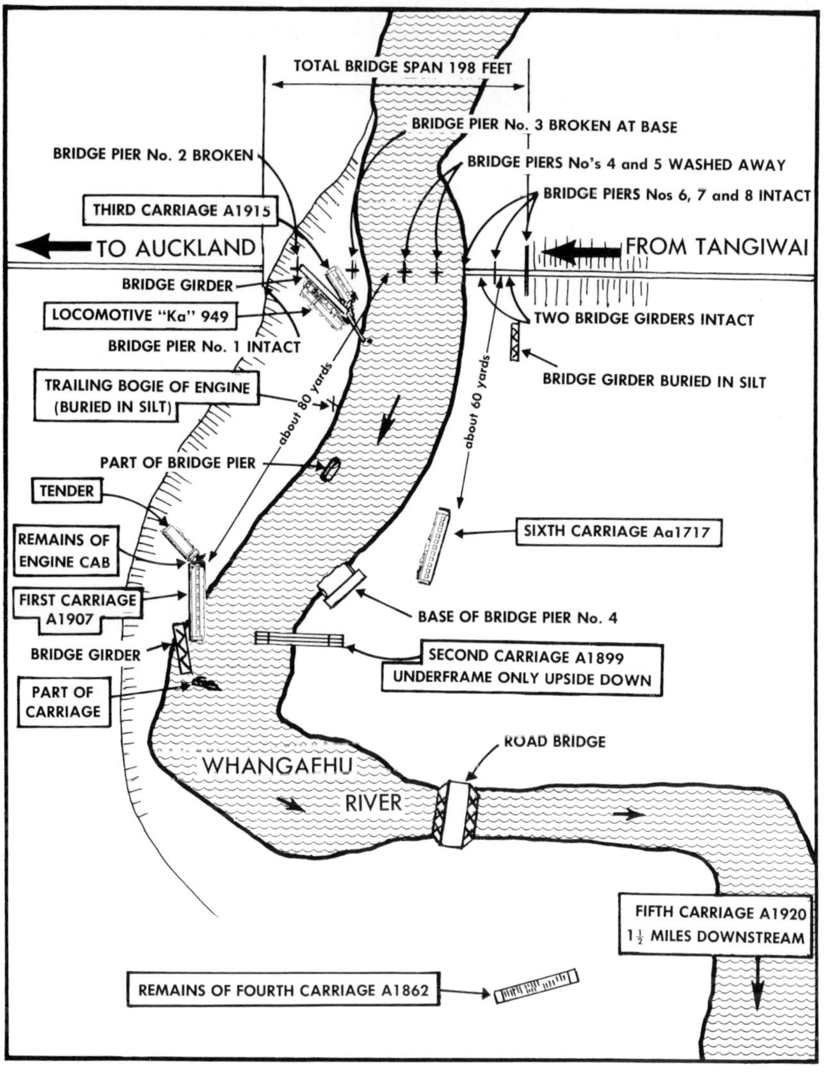

This diagram gives details of what happened to each unit of the train and to sections of the broken bridge after the lahar surged down the Whangaehu River on Christmas Eve 1953.

3. Travelled from Waiouru to Ohakune on the engine of the daylight limited express on 24 December 1953, passing over the bridge about 2.15 p.m., eight hours before the tragedy.

He had not observed anything unusual at the bridge on any of the these occasions.

The Railway Department's Research Engineer, P. B. Bryden, testified that the strength and stability of the superstructure and substructure of the bridge were ample for the heaviest loading carried and that the wrecking of the bridge could not be attributed in any way to failure under load of either girders or piers. Ability and judgement had been exercised in the design of the bridge, not only in the proportioning of the piers and spans, but also in determining the waterway provided, which was sufficient for any flood that could reasonably be expected. A fortnight later, the Engineer in Chief of the Ministry of Works, C. W. O. Turner, in effect endorsed Bryden's opinion. The choice of piers as the type of foundation was entirely suitable and even today it was possible that such piers would be used in rebuilding the bridge or constructing a bridge at a similar site. He judged the waterway allowed was reasonable and adequate, as indeed it had proved to be over the years, even including the recent happening.

Turner added: 'Since the disaster at Napier in 1931 engineers and architects have been designing and building structures which take account of [the effect of a major earthquake], but we do not blame those who built such structures before 1931 and, in my view, similarly no blame attaches to the engineers who designed, built and maintained the Whangaehu bridge before the disaster of Christmas 1953.'[21]

NO BLAME ANYWHERE

The board of inquiry found that no one directly or indirectly concerned could be blamed for the Tangiwai disaster. The accident was caused by the sudden release of a huge amount of water from the crater lake on Mount Ruapehu through an outlet cave beneath the Whangaehu Glacier. This was channelled down the Whangaehu River, carrying with it a high content of volcanic ash from the 1945 eruption and blocks of ice due to the collapse of large volumes of the glacier.

The flood, which could properly be termed a 'lahar', proceeded down the mountain as a wave, uplifting huge quantities of sand, silt and boulders. It was most violent and turbulent and of great destructive effect. It destroyed a portion of the railway bridge at Tangiwai before the arrival of the express, which was engulfed when crossing the bridge.

The board also found that railway engineers could not be held responsible for not taking steps to strengthen the Tangiwai bridge on the evidence of previous floodings of the Whangaehu River. The engineers, said the report, were in no position to assess, from past experience, the strength of the lahar that had caused the tragedy.

The board sought to clarify its position: 'Much of the evidence submitted relating to the order of events at the crucial time of the destruction of the bridge and of the train and of the conditions about the bridge, including the bed of the river, rests on inferences on which the board is asked to make findings of facts. It seems unavoidable that the reconstruction of some events and circumstances must rest on such a foundation, but the board has been careful since negligence is alleged to have regard to the cogency of such evidence.'[22]

The relative positions of the 13 m (42 ft) girder (span 3) and the first car (A 1907) dictated that the girder had been removed before the passage of the first car — either before the locomotive arrived on the span or while the locomotive and tender were going over the span. If this girder had been removed during the passage of the locomotive, there was a strong inference that some part of the heavy structure of the locomotive would have hit girder 2. There was, however, no evidence of extensive damage to girder 2 so it might therefore be inferred that girder 3 was not removed when the train went across it.

Span 3 had therefore been carried away before the locomotive moved on to it and it was most likely that pier 4 had been carried away before the train passed over it. This would have caused span 4 to be carried away. 'There is also a strong inference that pier 4 was removed by the lahar and that this caused the accident,' said the report. 'The removal of pier 5 at a later stage was partially a result, not a cause of the accident.'[23]

The board felt it might be advantageous if the general public had more understanding of the destructive nature of a lahar, so quoted approvingly from a report by James Healy, superintending geologist of the Geological Survey branch of the DSIR:

> A lahar is a type of mudflow that occurs in volcanic areas. Lahars may be formed by the waters of crater lakes being released by the collapse of the crater wall or by volcanic eruption, by the melting of snow and ice by volcanic heat, or by the action of rain on volcanic ash deposited on the steep slopes of volcanoes. They usually pick up large quantities of volcanic ash and other debris, and form a thick slurry that on account of its high density may carry even enormous boulders for many miles across fairly flat country once the initial momentum has been gained.
>
> [Board interpolation: "The flood from Ruapehu on the night of 24 December 1953 was of this type and is classed as a lahar."]
> The lahar at Tangiwai: The lahar reached Tangiwai about 10.10–10.15 p.m. in the form of a dense wave of water, sand and boulders. While the lahar passed there seems to have been little or no erosion and the shingle flat in which the river flows was smothered with a swiftly-moving mass of sediment. Above the railway bridge the flood spread out across the flats, depositing sand and boulders, and reached a depth of 20 ft at the bridge. It piled up to cross the highway and highway bridge, depositing sand and flooding across the highway for several hundred yards, and swept on down the river. Along the banks the vegetation was quickly buried by sand, but on the bed of the channel vegetation was flattened and abraded.[24]

Inspections of the river at various points, together with a study of the aerial photographs, confirmed the view that a large discharge from the lake had advanced to the railway bridge, slowed down only by bed resistance which had been increased by the high density of the lahar. If the crest had been advancing at an average spread of 16 km (10 miles) an hour, about 2½ hours would have elapsed from the time the waters were released until they arrived at Tangiwai at 10.17 p.m. It was established that the flow past the railway bridge had diminished considerably by 10.35 p.m.

A flood rise of 4.5–5 m (15–17 ft) had been measured at the railway bridge (i.e. above the bed as after flood) and slope area measurements gave a mean discharge of about 23,000 cusecs. This agreed with the general opinion that the peak discharge had been about 30,000 cusecs.

Beside the destruction of the road and railway bridges at Tangiwai, three further bridges had been destroyed, all within Waimarino County. It was not known for certain how far downstream the flood wave had moved in its original form, but it would have tended to flatten in the Whangaehu Valley proper owing to an increasing cross section and a very tortuous course. It was, however, significant that the steel underframe of car A 1920 — A on the train — had been carried about 2 km (1.2 miles) downstream from the railway bridge.

The flood was estimated to have arrived in the lower reaches at the State Highway bridge, Whangaehu, about 3.30 p.m. on 25 December 1953, a distance of about 110–130 km (70–80 miles) from Tangiwai. The flood rise had been between 1 and 1.25 km (3–4 ft) above normal river level. Observers had reported that the river was then very dirty and carried fairly large quantities of debris and logs, the timber being mostly willow. For comparative purposes it was recorded that a serious flood in the lower reaches of the Whangaehu River caused rises in the water level of up to 6 m (20 ft) or more.

Sand and boulders left by the flood on the left bank upstream from the railway embankment. The boulders were up to 1.25 m (4 ft) in diameter. In the foreground are remnants of the original vegetation, flattened and abraded by the force of the water.

Upstream from the Tangiwai railway bridge, large boulders had been deposited wherever the river had abruptly changed course. Many were up to 1.25 m (4 ft) in diameter and many were considerably bigger. Large quantities of material, generally described as sand, had been deposited and it was evident the river had been heavily laden with a mixture of boulders and sand. At these abrupt changes of course where the river had struck a bank or bluff some erosion had occurred, but it was comparatively small considering the height and violence of the flood indicating that the peak was of short duration.

Big boulders had evidently passed through the gap of the railway bridge, for two of the 5 tonne concrete blocks from the vicinity of pier 4 were to be seen some 55 m (60 yds) downstream from the road bridge, with a boulder of at least the same weight resting on top of them. There were numbers of boulders downstream from the railway and road bridges, but the mass did not extend far and even at the gorge a little downstream from the remains of car 1920 (A) the boulder deposit was small compared with that at and upstream from the railway bridge. On the reach approaching this gorge, however, enormous quantities of sand had been deposited.

The bridge was 60 m (198 ft) long, with massive concrete piers and abutments. It had been built about 1906 by the Public Works Department. Because files on the bridge had been destroyed in a Wellington fire there appeared to be no plan in existence showing how the bridge was actually constructed.

The first indication of damage to the bridge was on 23 January 1925 when, after a heavy swell, there was a fairly heavy scour on the upstream side of pier 4. In 1936, scouring had taken place at piers 3 and 4 and 15 wagons of stone had been used to build protection. In 1944 a hole had been scoured on the upstream side of pier 3, the hole being filled with stone. In June 1946, eight 5 tonne concrete protective blocks had been placed near pier 4.

Two of the eight protective concrete blocks placed around the foundations of piers 3 and 4 in 1946 were evidence of previous concern for the structural safety of these piers due to scouring.

After detailing the inspections made of the bridge before the accident, the board listed the damage caused on 24 December. Pier 2 had had the top portion broken off, pier 3 was smashed above the base into at least four pieces, pier 4 had been removed bodily and broken into three, the centre portion being 270 m (300 yds) downstream, while the top portion had not been located. Pier 5 had been completely carried off and broken into at least two pieces. The other piers, 1, 6, 7 and 8, were undamaged.

The board accepted the view that the waterway, the type of piers and the type and length of the spans were adequate for a design rainfall flood of 15,000 cusecs which, it held, was a reasonable estimate of the design rainfall flood; the intensity of past lahars provided no contrary evidence. The board found that the failure to design the bridge specifically to withstand the destructive effects of a lahar of the type which destroyed it was not due to lack of reasonable care. The board considered the lahar was of such nature and magnitude as to cause failure of a soundly constructed and maintained bridge. The repair work of 1925 had been carefully and competently executed; the then Chief Civil Engineer could reasonably assume the bridge would give no further trouble.

Of personnel, the board commented: '. . . in respect of every member of the train crew of train No. 626 and of every member of the Way and Works and Traffic Branches whose duties can be regarded as being involved in the accident there has been no failure to exercise reasonable care or fulfil any duty or responsibility reasonably to be expected of that member in the circumstances leading to the accident.'[25]

BOARD RECOMMENDATIONS

A suggestion made by a professional witness with prior experience in the Railways Department that a bridge division be created within the Chief Engineer's organisation to deal with the design, erection and maintenance of railway bridges, was commended.

Emergency equipment: Generally, the provision of emergency equipment in the guard's van was sufficient, but the board considered that in addition to the two kerosene and two hurricane lamps with a tin of fuel normally carried in the van there should be supplies of floodlights for emergency lighting. These could be plugged in at points provided in each individual carriage, operating off the battery equipment in each case.

New bridge: The board was satisfied that a new bridge with either one or three spans could be designed to provide a safe structure.

Luggage and postal vans: The board agreed with the department that it was not feasible to place these next to the engine.

Emergency exits: Provision of such exits in the roof of carriages would mean a major change in the structural design and there would be difficulty in keeping them weatherproof. They would need to be so tightly locked that it would possibly be more difficult to open them than to smash a carriage window. And if a carriage should be standing upright, a roof exit could be a danger in electrified areas.

Tangiwai station: Shifting the station nearer the bridge, having staff stationed at the bridge or building a tunnel under the river, should be considered more fully in relation to other possible safety measures.

Preventive steps: The board said that floats or ball cocks to operate a flood warning system were unsuitable for operation in a flood with a high solid content and any warning device attached to the bridge could fail if the warning was given when the train was at or near the bridge.

Any warning device relying on movement or collapse of the bridge piers or superstructure was dismissed as unsuitable, for the bridge could be dangerous without any actual movement.

The idea of operation of warning devices upstream was sound, but none actually suggested was suitable. The Railways Department was investigating the installation of a device in the

The new Tangiwai railway bridge crosses the Whangaehu River slightly upstream from the ruins of the original bridge. Should the water level of the river suddenly rise, a flood warning device on a pylon 12.5 km (8 miles) upstream triggers an alarm. The device is tested by each shift of Taumarunui train control, while there is a relay to the stationmaster's office at Waiouru in case of a communications failure with Taumarunui.

gorge, say 10 km above the bridge, on the principle of an activating force. Also being considered was a device using infrared rays which would strike a photo-electric cell on the other side. Any obstruction would allow the contact to drop, break it and give warning.

'Since Mount Ruapehu is not an extinct volcano, it would not be prudent to assume that the contents of the crater lake would always flow down the Whangaehu River,' the board said. 'Accordingly, it is recommended that warning devices should be installed at railway bridges over all streams between Waiouru and National Park.'[26]

Research: 'While witnesses have emphasised the need for the closest watch being kept on the level of the crater lake, and the condition of its outlet there are wider implications arising from the increasing knowledge of the dangers inherent in the presence of so large a volume of water at such a high level. . . . Moneys from the Earthquake and Disaster Funds might be made available to increase research into the characteristics of thermal activity in the mountain. This aspect we commend for consideration. . .'[27]

In the last sentence of the report, the board associated itself 'fully with the sentiments of sympathy extended by counsel and advocates to the relatives of those bereaved in this accident.'[28]

The number plate of Ka 949 has now been incorporated in a memorial at Tangiwai.

A simple ceremony on Christmas Eve 1963 marked the tenth anniversary of the tragedy at Tangiwai. In the glare of car headlights, more than 300 mourners stood silently with heads bowed as the Wellington to Auckland express crossed the Whangaehu River. Scores of passengers in the train stood in respect. It had been arranged that the wreath would not be dropped in the river on this occasion. As the train gathered speed north the railwaymen's tribute was recovered from where it had fallen and placed at the foot of a small white cross.

Scarcely anyone stops at Tangiwai these days. Cars slow down as they speed through the tiny village 688 m (2295 ft) up on the Waiouru Plains. Green grass grows along the riverbanks through the silt and the Whangaehu River tumbles ceaselessly down the rocky riverbed. The only visible reminder of the tragedy of Christmas Eve 1953 is a plaque at the site which records the accident.

But 11 km (7 miles) above the railway bridge is an electrode alarm system, installed in the bed of the Whangaehu River to give warning of floods. This system is monitored each shift by Taumarunui train control, as a routine precaution against another Ruapehu lahar. A back up is available in an electric water level recorder installed on the southern side of Mount Ruapehu, which would warn of the passage of a lahar in time for trains to be stopped.

Unknown victims of the disaster were buried in a common grave at the Karori Lawn Cemetery, Wellington, where their names and those of other victims are inscribed on a memorial tablet.

A 'living memorial' takes place each year, on Christmas Eve, when the Wellington to Auckland express slows to walking pace before crossing the Whangaehu River bridge at Tangiwai. From the cab the engine driver casts into the water a floral tribute as a token of remembrance from the New Zealand Locomotive Engineers', Firemen's and Cleaners' Association. The practice began at Christmas at 1954, and continues. Then, as now, a card with the flowers is inscribed: 'In memory of all who died at Tangiwai on Christmas Eve 1953.'

INQUEST EVIDENCE

Inquests into the deaths of 113 people whose bodies had been recovered from the Whangaehu River after the railway disaster were held in Wellington on 5 February 1954. The coroner, Mr W. G. C. Mellish, found the victims had died as a result of injuries suffered when the train plunged into the river just north of Tangiwai.

W. I. Inglis, guard on the express, described in his evidence how the train had passed Tangiwai at its normal speed. He was sitting facing the engine when suddenly the brakes were jammed on. They went on hard twice more and he was thrown first forward and then back, until the guard's van halted.

He grabbed his torch and jumped outside to see what was the matter. He saw another man with a torch running towards him, about three cars away. The man with the torch (who he later knew to be Mr A. C. Ellis) ran up and said: 'I tried to stop him, but he was going too fast. Half your train is in the river.' Inglis said: 'I couldn't believe it, but he kept saying, "It is, it is".'

The two men walked through the cars left on the rails. At the northern end of carriage Z, the door was open and the witness could see 'just 5 ft of rail stretching out into space'. There was water 6 ft (1.8 m) beneath it. Inglis then told the occupants to move out of the car into the back of the train, but before he himself had got to the middle the car began to saw. As the car toppled over into the river, he grabbed at a seat and then at the luggage rack. By that time the water was up round his armpits and the car was being carried down the river.

He smashed the nearest window with his torch and as the lights went out and the car toppled over onto its side, he clambered out. Then with some other unknown person he helped other occupants out.

In the meantime, persons on the riverbank had formed a human chain across to the carriage and all except one of its occupants were saved. He walked back to the train and put on the hand brakes.

Dr J. O. Mercer, pathologist at the Wellington Public Hospital, said some of the victims had been killed instantly, others had been drowned and many had fractured jaws and head injuries apparently from the train's sudden plunge forward. A curious point was the amount of silt that had been driven through soft parts of the skin and lodged against the bone, as for instance the flesh and bones of the skull. On the whole, said Dr Mercer, the main cause of death was drowning or asphyxiation by silt. There were also head injuries in 50 percent of those cases.

All text references, NZPA 5.2.1954.

DAMAGE TO RAIL BRIDGE

Pier 2 had the top portion broken off and this was lying under the bridge between piers 1 and 2.

Pier 3 was smashed above the base into at least four pieces. Two pieces were found near the locomotive, one between piers 2 and 3, but the remaining portion was not found.

Pier 4 was removed bodily and broken into three pieces. The base portion, weighing about 125 tonnes, came to rest 65 m (213 ft) downstream. The centre portion was found 275 m (900 ft) downstream, but the top portion was not located.

Pier 5 was removed bodily and broke into at least two pieces. The top portion was found 45 m (147 ft) downstream, but the lower portion was not located.

Piers 1, 6, 7 and 8 were not damaged.

Span 1 (6.5 m (21 ft) plate girders). This span was dislodged and the south end was thrown upstream.

Span 2 (13 m (42 ft) plate girders). This span was lying alongside the engine.

Span 3 (13 m (42 ft) plate girders). This span was on the right bank of the river about 73 m (240 ft) downstream, immediately downstream of and lying beside car A 1907.

Spans 4 and 5 (both 6.5 m (21 ft) plate girders). One span was lying on the left bank near the bridge and the other had not been located.

Spans 6 and 7 remained in place.

DAMAGE TO THE TANGIWAI RAILWAY BRIDGE
BEFORE 1953:

January 1925: Heavy swell, river rose about 2.75 m (9 ft) and left a heavy scour on the upstream side of pier 4, tilting this pier over about 12 mm (¼ in). Track bulged the same distance. Scour was filled with rock.

March 1936: Scouring at piers 3 and 4. Fifteen wagon loads of stone placed around these piers.

February 1944: River in high flood, a whirlpool scoured a hole 3 m (10 ft) in diameter and 1 m (3 ft) deep on the upstream side of pier 3. No damage was done to the foundations and the hole was filled in with stone.

June 1946: Eight 5 tonne concrete protective blocks were placed around pier 4.

Following the volcanic activity of Mount Ruapehu in 1946, the bridge was kept under close observation by the Railways Department.

In January 1948, the foreman of works reported he thought that if anything the creekbed was higher than when the concrete blocks had been placed in position and the blocks had not sunk at all. There was practically no water and sand was banked well up round piers 4 and 5 except on 4's river side where the main channel now flowed. The concrete blocks there were well out of the water and scour could be rated as nil since last inspected.

From this date until the disaster there was no record of damage.

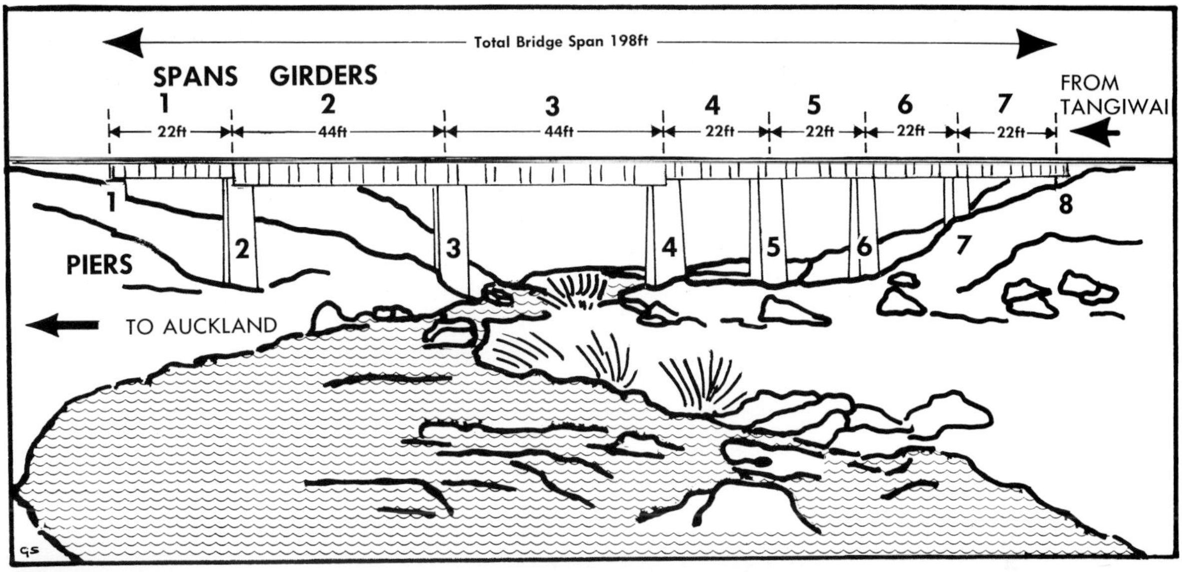

Above: The temporary railway bridge over the Whangaehu River opened on New Year's Day 1954.

Left: This view of the road bridge, looking upstream, shows how the abutment on the far bank, founded on sandstone, remained firm, while the near abutment was undermined by scouring.

WARNING GIVEN 30 YEARS BEFORE

In 1923, 30 years before the Tangiwai disaster, a sudden break in the wall of the crater lake on Mount Ruapehu caused a huge wave to sweep down the Whangaehu River. Estimates put the 1923 wave at 6 m (20 ft) high, the same height as that which struck and destroyed the bridge over which Ka 949 was drawing the 1953 express. But in 1923 the bridge held, though for months afterwards, while reinforcing and repair work were undertaken trains crawled over it at a snail's pace.

An even earlier freak flood was recorded by the Rev. Richard Taylor in his *New Zealand and its Inhabitants*, published in 1870. He wrote:

> The flood which occurred in the Whangaehu [*sic*] River on 13 December 1859 and carried away the recently erected bridge was of an extraordinary kind. This river takes its rise from the crater of Ruapehu, a snowy mountain, which forms the most conspicuous object of our landscapes; rushing thence along a snowy plain, it falls over a perpendicular cliff some 2000 ft into a deep chasm; the upper part of this huge wall is a mass of ice and even there this river appears to be a strong stream of milk white colour, being in fact diluted sulphuric acid.
>
> To account for this unexpected flood, which occurred in fine, dry, warm weather, it is most likely that a long continuance of heat detached a portion of this great cliff sufficient to arrest the course of the river and form a temporary lake, which, gradually rising in height, until its barriers were no longer able to resist the pressure, and then the whole volume of water, rushing along with immense impetus, carried the huge masses of ice and snow with it, as well as all the trunks of drift timber it met with in its passage; the flood overflowed the banks, depositing vast quantities of ice, snow and drift along the entire course, until it reached the bridge, which, considering the winding course of the river, must be nearly 100 miles distant. There the trunks and blocks of ice collected in such quantities that they were level with it and formed such a compact mass that an observer said it would have been quite possible to walk along the top of it across the river; the poor bridge creaked, opened and was swept away . . .
>
> The flood came down about 6 a.m. and in a little more than two hours it subsided, leaving large masses of ice, snow and mud, filled with crystals of ice, on the banks. The day being intensely hot, these heaps produced such a vapour as to appear like smoke, the ice and snow were remarkably compact, very black and emitting a strong sulphurous smell, and in such masses as actually to remain for nearly a week under the mud.

The name Tangiwai means 'weeping waters' or 'waters of sorrow', from *tangi*, to weep or lament; and *wai*, water. It was so named to commemorate the loss of a paramount chief who, according to legend, perished in a raging torrent that suddenly overwhelmed the normally placid crossing place in the Whangaehu River. (Fiordland greenstone is also known as tangiwai because the flecks in it resemble tears.)

Chapter 2

THE 10 WORST AFTER TANGIWAI

Railway accidents, especially those involving death, have always made headline news because they are rare.

The horrific Tangiwai disaster of Christmas Eve 1953 was by far New Zealand's worst, on every count, with 151 dead. Otherwise, in a marshalling of steam train accidents since 1880, fewer than half that number died in collisions, signal failures, slips, fog, speed or errors of judgement. This was in spite of the billions of kilometres recorded by passenger and goods trains keeping scheduled and run-as-required services, an unstable countryside, unpredictable weather prompting lahars, flooding, subsidences, slips and blinding fog, even stray animals wandering where they shouldn't.

Experience and its lessons, sometimes gleaned only in the wake of tragedy, merged with technological advances to help make the New Zealand Railways system one of the safest in the world. Indeed, it could be argued that rail in New Zealand is the safest form of transport in this country. Certainly the average passenger, whether on a long-distance express or a commuter facility, gives little thought to the possibility of running late, let alone being injured, or killed.

The emphasis on rail safety in all its aspects has been consistently upheld at every level of railways operations in New Zealand. The Westinghouse brake, couplings, the signalling system, vigilance devices — all have been improved through time and, in operation, checked and rechecked in the interests of user safety, even down to the intermediate train inspections made by train examiners (usually referred to as wheel tappers) at the principal stations between the original and terminal points of the train's journey.

Great credit should be paid to enginemen who, apart from being in command of a great iron monster of 145 tonnes working at a steam pressure of 90 kg (200 lbs) per 6.5 cm^2 (in^2) (or 13.8 kg per cm^2), hauling up to 12 to 18 carriages with up to 400–600 human bodies and rushing through the night, negotiate curves and reverse curves as tight as 150 m (7½ chains) in radius and land their precious freight safely at destination.

When the system fails — 'blinks' might be a better word — and an accident does happen, a thorough investigation is usually made not only to determine the cause of the accident but also to explore means of avoiding such mishaps in the future. The exception was sometimes made when the cause of the accident was plainly obvious as, for instance, a sudden landslide on a hitherto stable bank, or sudden flooding bringing subsidence of railway lines.

Boards of inquiry appointed under warrant by the Minister of Railways usually posed questions such as:

(1) What was the cause of the accident?

(2) Was any employee in the service of the Railways Department guilty of any dereliction of duty which directly or indirectly contributed to the accident?

(3) Generally, are there any circumstances in connection with the said accident which call for comment, particularly in respect of rolling stock and of the permanent way in the locality of the accident?

(4) What steps (if any) should be taken to prevent the occurrence of a similar accident?

The three-man tribunals had at hand background information, such as the composition of the train, tare weights and marshal order of the vehicles from the engine; the personnel of the train crew, with the guards (listed first), engine driver and fireman; and the running schedule.

Public sittings of a board of inquiry were advertised in appropriate newspapers and people desiring to give evidence were invited to do so. Engineering members of the tribunal usually visited the scene of the accident to inspect derailed vehicles (if still there) and the track.

Counsel involved in such an inquiry usually represented the Railways Department, the New Zealand Locomotive Engine Drivers', Firemen's and Cleaners' Association, the Amalgamated Society of Railway Servants, passengers with a vested interest in the result (such as injured passengers) and those appearing on behalf of relatives of dead passengers.

Evidence was taken on the point of derailment and a description of the accident plus operating conditions on the stretch of track where the accident happened. Then it was down to business, taking expert and other evidence, hearing counsel in cross-examination and putting specific queries. It was a matter of seeking the truth, not only in the interests of immediate justice but to try to ensure that defects or errors or wrong procedures could be corrected to make the Railways a still safer transport service.

Usually the tribunal considered possible causes of accident under half a dozen headings: obstruction on track, operating factors, excessive speed, defect in rolling stock, defect in engine, defect in track. Expert evidence usually resolved these questions.

(1) *Obstruction on track* was a self-evident issue. How long since another train had passed the accident point? How long since a ganger had patrolled or walked the section? Was there anything in the wreckage to raise a doubt? If nothing, the tribunal would record its opinion: 'We are therefore of the opinion that the accident was not caused by or contributed to

by the presence of an obstacle on the track.'
(2) *Operating factors.* How familiar was the engine driver with the section of line involved? How elastic was the timetable? Were operating schedules reasonable?
(3) *Excessive speed.* This was often the crunch issue, possibly the cause of the accident being investigated. Apart from passengers' opinions and those of the guard and eye witnesses, departmental engineers could usually calculate the speed of a train at the moment of accident, or near enough.

A first consideration was to establish positively the exact time the accident happened and, working back from that, to establish the times recorded passing stations immediately beforehand, having regard to speed or other restrictions, the nature of the run, the overturning speed of the engine, the momentum of carriages and other vehicles in the train and their position of rest, retardation due to braking, etc. Sometimes, in a bad accident, passengers' watches gave the exact time of accident, because they had stopped.

Many an engine driver, perhaps most, can 'feel' their speed and know when it is safe, so perform their duties subconsciously. Objects close to the line visible in good conditions enable a driver to consciously estimate his speed, something not, of course, possible in darkness or fog, conditions conducive to accident. Other drivers judge speed by the sound of clicking over the rail joints, while the beat of the engine is another aid. A last test to determine speed is a practical repetition of the run made just before the accident, with a comparison of times.
(4) *Defect in rolling stock.* Evidence was always called on the periodical overhauls of the rolling stock and of the inspections made before the dispatch of the train on the run on which the accident happened.
(5) *Defect in engine.* Similarly, overhaul and inspection records were produced.

Possible causes nos 4 and 5 would seem to be merely a procedural precaution — how often has a fault been found in rolling stock? Maintenance of railway engines and rolling stock in New Zealand is exceptional by world standards. Steam boiler inspections were thorough, to the point where New Zealand Railways never had a boiler explosion, something not uncommon in the United States, Britain and other places overseas. Still, against a most remote possibility, something could have gone wrong so evidence was needed and weighed.

Quite early on, at the beginning of the 1870s, New Zealand engineers began designing their own locomotives for overseas construction and towards the end of the 1880s locomotives began to be built in New Zealand, to establish a flourishing, expert industry. So New Zealand engineers knew what they were about when it came to diagnosing possible engine defects.
(6) *Defect in track.* This could be a complex subject, and sometimes a successful avenue in seeking to determine the cause of a derailment. 'The importance of track maintenance in relation

to speed cannot be overstressed,' wrote one board of inquiry (Haywards, 1943). 'To begin with, the engineering members of the board carefully inspected the track in the vicinity of the scene of the accident and particularly that portion of it immediately before the point of derailment. We then examined the carefully recorded measures of the track made by the Chief Engineer immediately after the accident. The study of these measurements, chiefly in relation to curvature, cant, slack and wear on rails, proved to be most instructive to the board.'[1] (In this instance, the board of inquiry had identified its proper target, duly finding, among other returns, defects in the track.)

On rare occasions a board of inquiry had to suspend its sessions while justice took a turn, by arraigning an engine driver and sometimes his fireman before a criminal court. The human element was always the touchpoint, something which just could not be securely guarded against. Yet thousands of train crew, engineers, firemen and guards, who have worked for the New Zealand Railways, have never been touched by doubt, faltered in their routine, or failed to rise to meet emergencies. Only very rarely did someone let the side down, sometimes sadly with disastrous consequences.

This perhaps explains why a board of inquiry into a railway accident so often approached its task with an evident suspicion that the engine crew had had one over the eight (or perhaps just eight), and why, almost always, the suspicions were dismissed out of hand, and recorded accordingly.

Typical, though particularly thorough, was this board of inquiry verdict:

> After the accident a number of rumours gained currency and circumstantial statements were made by witnesses regarding the subject matter of these rumours. In particular it was suggested that a third man travelled in the engine, that alcoholic liquor was consumed on the engine by the engine crew and that an emergency signal of three whistles for brakes was given immediately before the accident occurred. We have fully investigated the grounds for these rumours and statements and are completely satisfied they are unfounded. We find specifically that no person except the members of the engine crew travelled on the engine at any stage of the journey, that no alcoholic liquor was consumed by the members of the engine crew while they were on duty and that they were not in any way under the influence of alcohol when they booked on for duty.[2]

In less medically sophisticated years there was the danger of sudden collapse, a coronary perhaps, to paralyse an engine driver and, if discerned in time, to invite emergency action from his fireman. Once or twice the corrective action seems to have come too late. Now the workhorse railcars used everywhere have vigilance devices, even the 'deadman's pedal', while medical inspections are part of Railways routine.

Steam had another hazard, that of smothering train crews and passengers in tunnels. Rank-smelling smoke, with its liberal load of smuts, bounced off tunnel walls and came into

Locomotive F 224 was the victim of a wash-out early in her career.

carriages where passengers had not wound up windows. One runaway train which ran through points and smashed the samson block was carrying an unconscious engine crew who, fortunately, survived the smash. They were not the only crew to be threatened or overcome in tunnels.

Aside from slips, subsidences or floodwaters, in the main unexpected and often unavoidable, the main cause of steam railways accidents was centred on the signalling system. Now this is usually the single-lens searchlight, the single green go-ahead. An engine crew is never colour blind. Only a once in a lifetime mechanical defect, or climatic impact (very hot sun, very hard frost), could threaten a signal failure. Other times failure was the product of the human element. Now, indeed, only the human element can cause a fault in sophisticated built-in safeguards.

Train accidents can still happen, but they are increasingly the exception, the rarity. How long since newspapers splashed headlines reporting rail fatalities? There can be the inevitable crossing accident, in spite of barrier arms, alarm bells and flashing red lights, but another Tangiwai? another Ongarue? another Hyde? It is highly improbable.

Tangiwai was the worst, the horrible, tragic freak, the ultimate in railway disaster, but the next 10 worst railways disasters in New Zealand, measured by the toll of dead and injured, happened more than a generation ago. They offer us lessons from the past.

Rimutaka Incline 11 September 1880

'They lay around for a time unconscious and those who first recovered their senses described the scene as a fearful one — killed and wounded lying around in all directions covered with blood, and the train above suspended in mid-air, threatening every moment to fall on them.'[1] This was a newspaper summary of the plight of passengers catapulted from two carriages blown in 1880 by a gale-force wind blast from a vulnerable rail point on the rugged Rimutaka mountain range that divides Wellington from the Wairarapa.

Fortunately the Fell locomotive held to its central rail traction, proving strong enough to hold two passenger cars and a luggage van in suspension over the deep ravine at a point known as the Siberia Curve. When the Fell brake van at the rear of the train was detached to coast down the incline for help, the other two produce vans, full of timber, tipped over and also hung suspended by their couplings.

Three children died and 21 people were injured, many seriously, in this sad 1880 accident, the first major train accident on New Zealand railways and the first fatal accident on the Rimutaka incline.

This 4.8 km (3 mile) incline railway was an engineering feat, sometimes claimed to be unique in the world of railways. When opened in 1878 it brought rich Wairarapa farmlands and forests into economic communication with Wellington and allowed passengers to relax in the snug comfort of a railway saloon, while specially designed Fell mountain-climbing locomotives, which gripped an elevated centre-rail between the running tracks, puffed and pounded up the steep gradients in all weathers. The H class Fell locomotives were inserted into the train to propel it up the incline, partly in the interests of safety, partly to protect passengers from smoke residue.

Because the railway between Cross Creek and the Summit crossing this section of the Rimutaka Range was required to ascend a grade of 1 in 15 for almost 5 km (3 miles), a special type of locomotive, designed by English inventor John Barraclough Fell, was adopted for this line. Fell's patent employed a large double-headed rail laid sideways on pedestals located in the centre of the track between the running rails. The horizontal driving wheels were brought to bear against each face of the centre-rail by means of powerful springs. This no doubt held the Fell engine on the rails on 11 September 1880.

Because of this steep grade, all trains were restricted to a gross load of 260 tonnes, requiring a minimum of four locomotives, each capable of hauling 65 tonnes. The engines also had to be marshalled throughout the train ahead of its scheduled 65 tonnes. The four Fell engines originally imported, apart from having departmental numbers H 199, H 200, H 201 and H 202, were named Mount Cook, Mount Tongariro, Mount Egmont and Mont Clenis.

On the day of the accident at Siberia, only one Fell engine

An artist's exaggerated impression of the Rimutaka incline tragedy which was published on the front page of the *Australasian Sketcher* of 9 October 1880.

was working the train, which was marshalled as follows: two passenger cars and a goods van, propelled by the Fell engine, were leading, followed by two loaded goods wagons, then a special Fell brake van — a gross total of about 60 tonnes.

On 11 September 1880 the morning train to Wellington was making good time on the way to the Summit from Featherston. Two four-wheeled composite carriages led the train (the Fell engine was in the middle of the train, propelling as well as pulling) and the carriages were full of families travelling to Wellington for the weekend. Driver George Bartley would have been well satisfied with the train's progress.

As the train cleared a deep rocky cutting and rounded a 100 m (5 chain) radius curve on an open embankment spanning a gully known as Siberia 1200 m (60 chains) from the Summit, gale-force winds struck, mounting to a fatal gust with an estimated velocity of just under 200 km (120 miles) an hour.

A survivor, the Rev. Gossett, remembered two fierce gusts, the first hurling a shower of stones against the carriage, the second strong enough to blow the carriages off the line. Henry Dunn told how he had been standing outside on the platform of the first carriage when, some 136 m (150 yds) before the second tunnel, the wind blew the carriage bodily off the rails. He was tossed off. In the second carriage, which had been thrown over on its side, passengers were catapulted together, some being severely injured.

The engine remained firm, tightly gripping the vital middle rail, although swaying visibly under the strain. The whole of the upper part of the first carriage was smashed into matchwood and hurled over the precipice. Passengers and debris were scattered among boulders down the side of the gully, but they did not fall to the bottom, about 30 m (100 ft) down.

Passengers recovered their senses in a scene of total catastrophe, buffeted by the gale and ever threatened by the carriages and vans suspended in mid-air above them.

One who responded immediately was the incline brakesman, Michael Berry, who immediately uncoupled the Fell brake van at the rear of the train and piloted it down the incline by its own momentum to seek aid at Cross Creek. These four-wheeled brake vans were used to check the braking of trains while descending the incline.

Survivors helped the injured to a nearby cutting, where they sheltered waiting for the special rescue train, safe now from the looming threat of the suspended rolling stock which, still buffeted by the wind, threatened to pull the engine over, or snap the couplings, or even to tear the middle rail from its track. Rescuers found the force of the wind so great that doctors and helpers had to crawl on their hands and knees, tightly clutching the middle rail, to avoid being blown over the precipice. Three children lay dead and 21 people were injured, some seriously. It was not considered safe to allow the relief train to stand on the embankment, so it was parked in the tunnel.

At an inquest held at Featherston four days after the accident, the jury found the deaths had been accidental, caused by the carriages being blown off the railway line. No

Breakwind fences subsequently erected at Siberia curve on the Rimutaka incline. This picture clearly shows the elevated centre-rail.

A contemporary newspaper sketch purporting to illustrate the accident at the Siberia curve on the Rimutaka incline after all rolling stock except the locomotive was blown off the rails.

Two sturdy little Fell locomotives push the Royal train around Siberia curve during the visit of the Queen and the Duke of Edinburgh in 1954.

blame was attached to anyone, jurors said, but immediate action was urged to construct wind shelters or other protective means on dangerous parts of the incline.

Soon afterwards breakwinds were built at Siberia and at other places on the line prone to excess wind. These remained until the incline was closed in October 1955 when the Rimutaka tunnel and deviation were opened. Strangers who questioned the purpose of these high wooden fences when travelling the incline and wondered if their legs were being pulled, were sometimes convinced when, on their return journey, fine weather degenerated into gale-force winds from the north-west.

The other important consequence of the tragedy was that two engines were thereafter used if the wind was fierce. As the trains grew longer, with increased traffic, extra locomotives were inserted, sometimes up to five, each being attached in front of its share of the load.

Fifty-six years later, on 9 October 1936, a north-west gale struck again. A railcar travelling south between Featherston and Pigeon Bush was blown off the rails just before reaching a section of the line sheltered by a large wooden breakwind. The force of the wind was estimated at 128 km (80 miles) an hour. When the railcar crashed over on to its side, the passengers were thrown out of their seats. One woman was hurled over the top of three seats in front of her. Seven of the eight people injured were women. The unexpected velocity of the wind was once again the sole cause of the accident.

A Fell locomotive and a Fell van, on a happier occasion.

The railcar *Mamari* after being blown off the rails near Featherston. The large wooden breakwind is on the right.

Rakaia 11 March 1899

'Jump for your lives!' echoed from the bleak rain-soaked station platform at Rakaia on the evening of 11 March 1899. Seconds later a packed excursion train crashed into the rear of a much larger companion train, for both were bringing day picnickers home. Three young women and a child were killed and 22 people injured in the accident, which raised public and Parliamentary controversy over the signalling and braking efficiency of the Railways service.

Three thousand people had travelled from Christchurch to Ashburton for the annual picnic of employees of the Islington freezing works. A south-west gale which brought with it driving rain had made conditions unpleasant, so they were tired and wet excursionists who duly left on their return journey in the two special trains.

The first, drawn by two locomotives, Ub's 287 and 279, hauled a load of 30 carriages and a guard's van. This train left Ashburton at 6.05 p.m. The second train consisted of one locomotive, Ub 284, 14 carriages, two wagons and a guard's van. Supposed to leave at 6.05 p.m., this train did not clear the platform until 6.35 p.m. because two wheels of a van had derailed.

The guard's van (right) was rammed hard into the last two carriages, which were telescoped into each other. The roof of one carriage lies along the top of the other. The hole in the side of the carriage was cut away with axes to remove the four bodies.

So great was the crush on the Ashburton platform, aggravated by some degree of intoxication, that the chief guard, William Climpson, after giving the start signal by blowing a whistle and extending his hand, was unable to reach his van. He was left behind, leaving only a porter acting as assistant guard on the train.

The first excursion train reached Rakaia and drew up on the south side of the platform, where it had to wait for the evening train from Christchurch to Ashburton to cross. This train was about 20 minutes late, so the first excursion train could not get away until the second excursion train hove into sight. In addition, the Methven branch train was standing on a branch line to the south of Rakaia Station.

With the first excursion train parked in assumed security at the south Rakaia platform, the second train drove at more than usual speed as engine driver Charles Henry Carter tried to make up his 20 minute lag. Such action was expected by the Railways authorities, though always within the limits of safety.

Should this train have been allowed to proceed without its senior guard? The Ashburton stationmaster was concerned, to the point of telegraphing ahead to Chertsey and Rakaia. He got no response from Chertsey, perhaps because the stationmaster was busy on the platform, so driver Carter drove his train unchecked on to Rakaia, and disaster.

Perhaps guard Climpson's absence was not material, for his assistant, Joseph John Burrow, was relieved of his ticket-collecting duties so he could attend to signals. The secretary of the picnic committee, C. E. Fisher, arranged for two committee men to collect tickets, while an Islington works butcher, V. J. Fitzpatrick, was assigned to help Burrow in the guard's van at the rear of the train. They were there when the train passed Chertsey, where the stationmaster showed a green light, indicating 'All right'.

But was everything all right? Secretary Fisher thought the train was travelling too fast and pointed this out to guard Burrow, who also noted how the van was swinging 'considerably'. He put out his green light signal to the fireman, swinging it clear of the van. The meaning was 'Caution — go on slowly — stop at station signal'. But he had no acknowledgement, perhaps because of the torrential rain, perhaps because of trailing smoke which clouded the lee side of the train. So as the train drove towards Rakaia Burrow, with the help of his passenger-assistant Fitzpatrick, put on the van brake.

Rakaia railways staff knew the second excursion train was on its way, having been warned by Ashburton. They also knew the train should stop automatically at the Rakaia station points until the signal was given to come in. As an added precaution, however, and because there was no signal down from the station, station clerk James O'Neill was sent to the points with a warning red signal lamp and he was in position in time to signal the train to stop. He was some 270 m (297 yds) from the station.

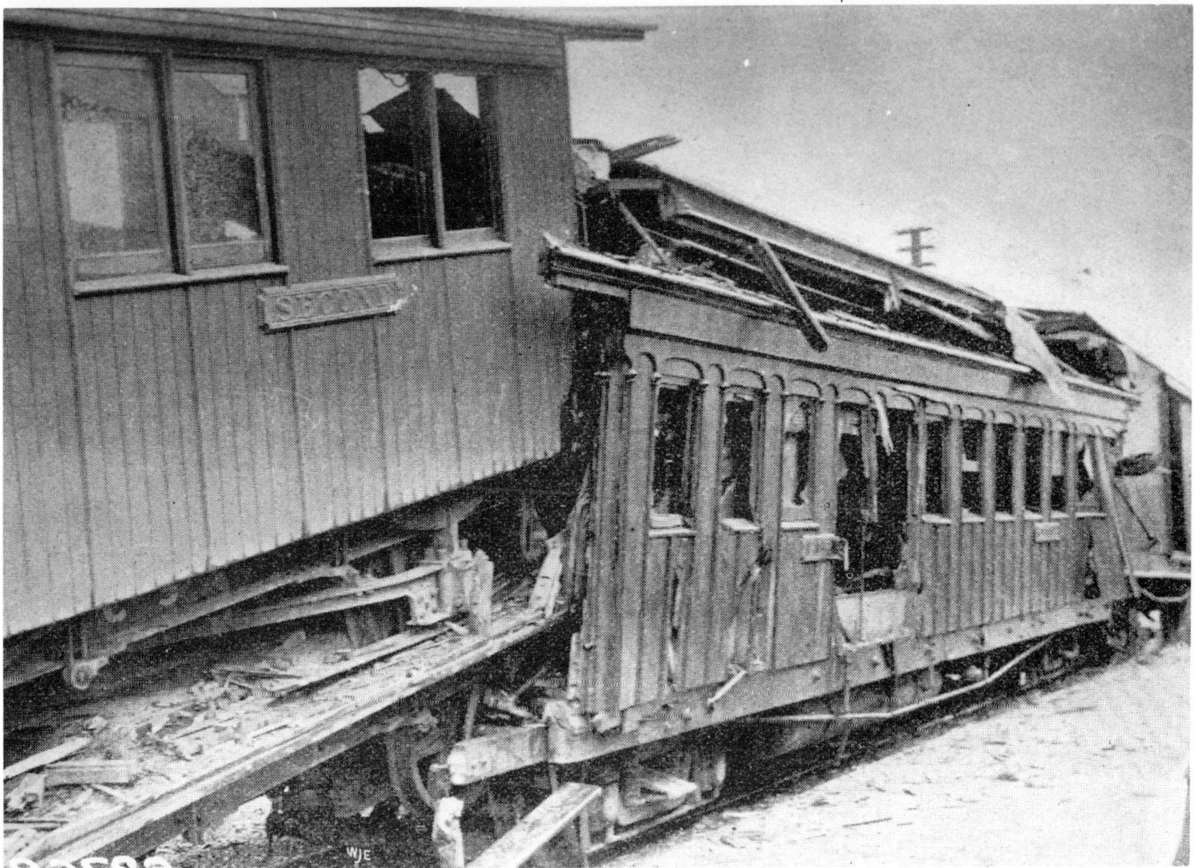

Although the first excursion train had begun moving ahead from the Rakaia station when the rear-end collision occurred, the force of the impact is graphically illustrated in this picture. The third to last carriage (upper left) was thrown high and it smashed to pieces the second to last carriage (lower left), leaving only the underframe and wheels. The roof of this car lies along the top of the last carriage (centre). Both the third and second to last carriages were pitched up on an angle as the last carriage sustained the violent force of the smash. The guard's van is at the extreme right.

Driver Carter saw the red light warning and gave three short sharp whistles, the signal for 'down brakes'. Immediately the assistant guard in the van at the end of the train complied, helped by the passenger Fitzgerald who, seeing sparks from the wheels of the van, concluded that the brake had been applied when passing the emergency signal. The screw brake on the tender was applied by the fireman shortly after the driver had turned off the steam and applied his own brake, sand being used freely after the engine wheels had skidded at least once. Shortly after applying the airbrake the engine driver reversed his engine.

The brakes failed to hold because the heavy rain, impelled by a strong south-west wind, had made the rails slippery. The lights of the rear of the first excursion train, stationary at Rakaia station, were just visible to the fireman when driver Carter reacted to the emergency signal and they came increasingly into focus as the locomotive moved inexorably towards them.

The crash, when it came, completely telescoped the guard's van and the three carriages next to it.

Even more serious damage would have resulted but for the prompt action of J. Curson, the guard on the first train. When he saw that a crash appeared inevitable, he signalled to his engine drivers, Gardiner and Hyland, to move on. They

The third to last carriage (right), telescoped on top of the second to last carriage at Rakaia station.

applied steam but the great weight of the train meant it moved only two carriage lengths before the accident.

That the damage was restricted to the van and only three carriages was undoubtedly due to the first train being on the move, however slowly. Had it remained stationary the danger to passengers in all 30 carriages (most of which were filled to capacity) would have been appalling. As it was, passengers from the last three or four carriages standing on the platform anticipated the accident by crying, 'Jump for your lives!', a timely warning which saved more lives.

William Hyland, driver of locomotive Ub 279, the second engine on the first excursion train on the night of the tragedy. Hyland saved many lives by starting his train promptly, so cushioning the impact.

When the huge locomotive heading the 200 tonne train crashed into the guard's van, at a reduced speed of about 30 km (20 miles) an hour, it stove one end in as far as the bogie under the carriage. The van in turn was driven into the second-class compartment of an American carriage. The next carriage, one of the 'old-fashioned' cars, was crushed by the third to last carriage, which rode right up over the top, leaving nothing but the floor and the wheels of the second to last carriage, the whole body being crushed to matchwood.

Some panic ensued, some men fighting with women and children to escape from the wrecked carriages. The cries of the injured spurred efforts to free the trapped, and axes were used to break into the sides of the carriages. Strangely, the first two carriages behind the engine of the second excursion train were only slightly damaged, no more than the couplings being broken. Two carriages on the northbound express were made into ambulance wagons while a room at the Rakaia Post Office was converted for use as a hospital.

At an inquest into the deaths of the four passengers, guard Burrow told how he had got on to the front carriage nearest the engine as the train started and begun collecting tickets. Told that his senior officer, guard Climpson, had missed the train,

The locomotive of the second excursion train, Ub 284, after repairs and a complete overhaul, was used to haul the Royal train between Christchurch and Dunedin during the visit in 1901 of the Duke of Cornwall and York (later King George V).

he immediately went to the van, where he could control the brake. In due course he signalled the 'Caution — go on slowly — stop at station signal' to the engine crew. F. D. Mather, fireman on the train, said he had not seen the signal, though he had looked towards the van at least twice. He further affirmed that the locomotive and tender were the only vehicles on the train equipped with the Westinghouse air brake.

The jury brought in a verdict that the accident had been caused by the negligence of Charles Henry Carter, the driver of the second excursion train, 'in maintaining too high a rate of speed and thereby not having sufficient and proper control over his train in approaching the Rakaia station'. The jury went further, drawing attention to 'the lack of proper and necessary signalling appliances at such an important station as Rakaia'.[1] On the night in question, five passenger trains met and the only method of signalling was by dispatching a messenger up the line with a hand lamp. (A small red lantern held by a rain-drenched clerk at the side of the track had been the only warning of danger.)

Other conclusions concerned the absence of continuous brakes on passenger trains, the want of judgement on the part of the Ashburton stationmaster in not causing the second excursion train to be stopped at Chertsey so the driver might be informed of the absence of the head guard, and a commendation for the prompt action of the officials of the first excursion train in moving it forward, 'thereby avoiding a much more serious calamity'.

The verdict was equivalent to one of manslaughter, so driver Carter stood trial in the Supreme Court in Christchurch. He was acquitted, but for Charles Carter this was not the end. A Royal Commission followed and, when the findings were released, he was dismissed from the service. Was he a scapegoat for a railway system suffering from severe growing pains, using operational methods that had not kept pace with increased traffic? Certainly many safety measures were introduced in the ensuing years — fixed signals, the tablet system and the Westinghouse brake throughout entire trains. All stemmed from the Rakaia disaster.

Charles Henry Carter, driver of the second excursion train which crashed into the rear of the first excursion train at Rakaia station on 11 March 1899.

Footnote: Many years later Charles Henry Carter was given a full pardon.

Whangamarino 27 May 1914

Tablet porter William Donaldson was alert, as always, when he signalled a northbound 41-truck freight train into a siding at Whangamarino station, 11 km (7 miles) south of Mercer, at 4.45 a.m. on 27 May 1914. The train was running late, but as Donaldson swung the siding points and then sat on the switch to allow the engine and trucks to pass from the main line, he knew all was well. The northbound Wellington to Auckland express, though running slightly ahead of time, would be held by the red home signal on the semaphore 550 m (604 yds) south of the station.

The leisurely goods train and the scheduled express often crossed at Whangamarino, the only difference tonight being that it was the coldest night of the year so far and that fog hung low. It was a more or less routine situation — until, out of the night, its headlights blasting the darkness, roared the express, right on top of him.

William Donaldson was thrown down the side of the track, unconscious, as the express locomotive ploughed into that part of the freight train still being pulled from the main line, smashing the last trucks to pieces. Nor did the express escape damage. While the engine ploughed off the rails, to overturn, the following mail van broke its coupling and almost com-

The interior of the sleeping car of the express after the wrecked compartment had been cleared of debris. The floor and one wall of the telescoping mail van are on the left. The left-hand wall of the carriage was completely torn away by the front end and floor of the van.

Left: One of the injured passengers being carried from the scene of the wreck.

Above: Where death came to three men — the telescoped sleeping car (left) and the mail van of the express.

pletely telescoped into the adjoining sleeping car. Three passengers in this carriage died and five others were seriously hurt.

At the rear end of the express, people did not realise anything was amiss. But those at the sharp end, passengers and train crew, groping in the darkness for information and on rescue work, knew that something was terribly wrong. For it was quickly confirmed that the semaphore light was green, giving the express clear passage between 40 and 48 km (25 and 30 miles) an hour past the non-stop Whangamarino station.

Everybody, it seemed, had done everything correctly. The express engine driver and fireman had seen the green go-ahead signal and continued forward. The driver of the freight train had responded to Donaldson's own green light and swung his train into the siding.

Donaldson, who had come on shift at 10 p.m. at this sole charge station, had the southern signal set at danger to stop a train just before midnight. After putting the signal to safety and allowing the train to proceed, he put it back to danger again. The signal was working correctly and he noticed no irregularity in the back light of the signal. As no train was expected before the main trunk express, the signal lever was left at danger and locked, the key being placed in the station building. His other duties included tending lamps in the station.

Freight train No. 81 from Mercer was running half an hour late but it had no scheduled time for arriving at Whanga-

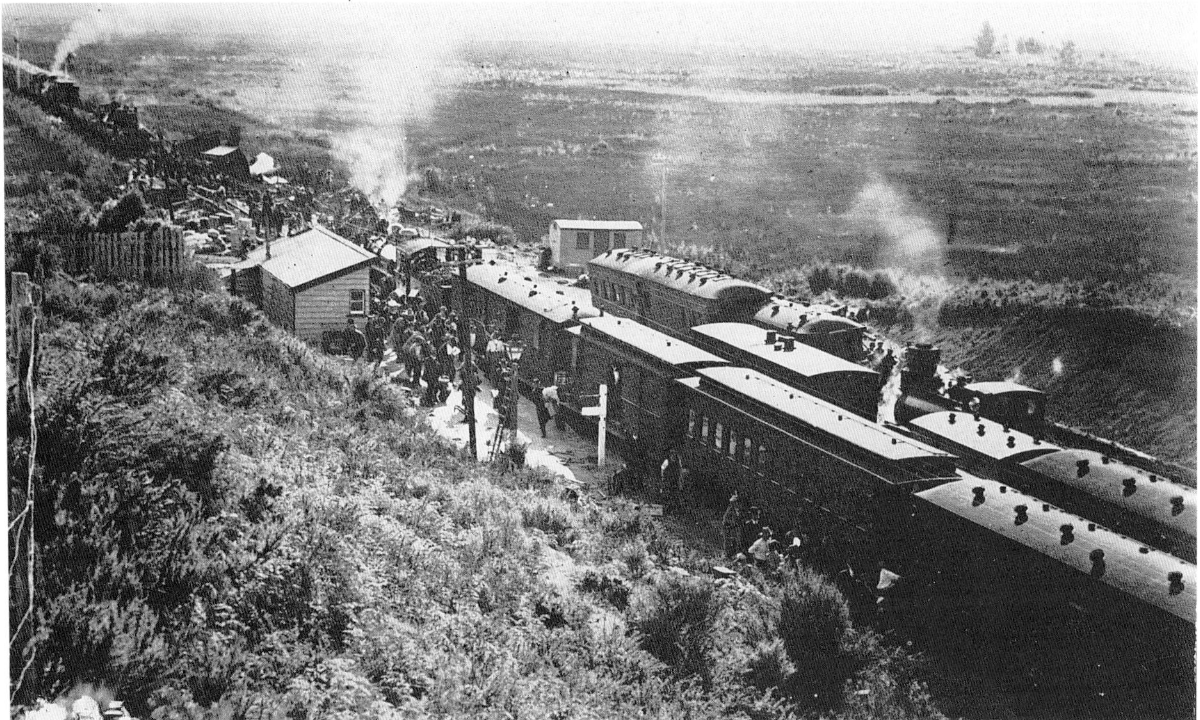

Whangamarino station a few hours after the Wellington express had crashed into a shunting goods train, killing three passengers in the sleeping car. The wreckage lies beyond the station. Travellers from Rotorua are transferring to another train to complete their journey to Auckland.

marino; it all depended on the size of the train. Usually the express was timed to pass the freighter at Te Kauwhata but Whangamarino was an alternative point of crossing. So when Donaldson heard the freight train approaching he unlocked the points to feed it on to the siding. Next he was lying unconscious beside the track some distance away, his arm fractured, buried under debris.

He said later: 'My first intimation of the approach of the express was seeing its headlights a few yards away from me. I cannot say I heard the crash of the collision and I remember nothing about the incident.'[1] But he did remember seeing the white back light of the southern signal when clearing the southbound train about midnight and that fog had obscured his view when preparing for the crossover. And he had not walked down the line to get a view.

The point became crucial, because the tablet porter or other Railways officers in charge of the signal were required to frequently and carefully observe its working, including confirming the back light when the signal was set to danger — red.

A small bull's eye let into the back of the signal lamp, to show a white light called the back light, reacted to a metal shutter which moved with the signal arm. If set in the danger position, a trifling drop in the signal arm would raise the shutter sufficiently to obscure the back light. The absence of this light would immediately indicate to the officer responsible for the signal either that the lamp had gone out or that the full danger signal was not properly displayed. If it was obscured by fog or mist, the officer was obliged to walk towards the signal until he could see it. This Donaldson had not done. In

The telescoped mail van (foreground) and sleeping car in which three passengers were killed.

his defence, witnesses — including the crew of the express train — confirmed that the platform pull-over control lever at the station was locked and set at danger. What had gone wrong?

The question was urgent because a ghastly wreckage had resulted. Although about two-thirds of the long goods train had passed over the points on to the siding, the collision completely shattered an empty horse box in the direct path of the express engine and eight empty sheep or cattle trucks were destroyed. The guard's van at the rear of the goods train was not damaged, guard J. J. Doyle reporting only a slight bump at the moment of impact. Yet, had there been another minute to spare, the whole of the goods train would have cleared the main line. For 45 m (50 yds) down the line there was a carpet of splintered wood and twisted iron.

The mail van behind the express locomotive pierced the heavily built sleeping carriage as though the structure was cardboard, shattering one wall and the internal partitions with their heavy furniture and crushing passengers among the wreckage. The main direction of the telescoping action was slightly towards the corridor side of the sleeper, with the result that the wall on that side was crushed, the lower part being forced outwards while the upper part, turning inwards, was shattered. A space of about 0.5 m (2 ft) remained between the walls on the other side and into this interval several of the passengers were crowded. Others were driven forward in the mass of smashed woodwork which piled up as the carriage body drove through the internal partitions. Steam was shut off the express train at the time of collision and the fireman was preparing to exchange tablets.

John Stone, driver of the express, was not worried when he saw the headlights of a train on the siding about six or seven engine lengths away, because it was usual for the train to be there or on some other siding. When the freight engine gave three whistles — the danger signal — he applied the emergency brakes immediately, reducing the speed of his train to about 25 km (15 miles) an hour. He thought, 'The only thing I can do is hang on.'[2] So both Stone and his fireman, F. G. Pardington, stuck to their posts in the locomotive as it ploughed forward and were fortunate to be thrown out uninjured when the locomotive fell off the embankment, 55–65 m (60–70 yds) past the point of initial collision.

Among the 11 passengers and one attendant in the sleeping car was W. J. Hill, a *New Zealand Herald* reporter, who filed this report to his paper:

> I was only dozing when the express ran across the Whangamarino swamp. The first warning of disaster was a grinding crash, followed by the splintering of glass. Then came a succession of crashes, apparently caused by the shattering of the wooden partitions as the postal van ploughed through the sleeper. The train bumped and jolted severely and then came to a standstill. As it stopped it seemed as if the whole carriage had collapsed upon us. The lights were extinguished by the shock and we were left in darkness, ignorant of what had happened and confused by ignorance of what might happen.
>
> I tried to move but found my shoulder was pinned by part of the carriage wall and other wreckage. Someone called out, "strike a match," but others shouted a warning as gas was escaping and filling the car.
>
> "I have been in a smash before and if anyone strikes a light there's no hope for us," someone exclaimed. For what seemed a long time, everyone lay still, until the silence was broken by groans. One of the passengers called out, "My God, lift this up".
>
> Then I managed to get out of my bunk and found Mr Borrie, who had been sharing my cabin, already standing up. In every direction our hands encountered woodwork. I found a boot, and one of the other men took it from me, and smashed the only window that was at all clear. Then we cleared away most of the broken glass and crawled out.[3]

Passengers in other carriages felt the shock so slightly they thought the train had merely pulled up, so it was some time before they alighted to gather about the wreckage. Then they went to work with a will, joining those who had escaped injury in the damaged carriage and forced their way to freedom. Rescue work was hampered because there was only one lamp, that carried by the guard, and it was not immediately possible to appreciate the full extent of the disaster.

Two men were groaning and because it was necessary to cut the debris away, piece by piece, it was nearly 8 a.m. before the last passenger was found. After half an hour's labour the body of Orton Stevens was brought out. General manager in New Zealand of the National Mutual Life Association, he was also a

The capsized express locomotive A 584 lying among the wrecked wagons in swampland at the side of the track just north of Whangamarino station, which can be seen in the background.

former Mayor of Lower Hutt. He was unlucky in that he had asked the sleeping car attendant to shift him from a four-berth cabin to a two-berth cabin in the centre part of the carriage, a move which cost him his life. Charles Peterson, on a holiday visit from Melbourne, was the last person recovered. An iron bar pinning him by the neck was removed, to his sigh of relief, but he died quite soon. The third fatality, George Grimstone, of Wellington, heard the crash before the walls of the carriage came in on him. Then he became unconscious. He died in the Waikato Hospital the same day.

Jammed in the wreckage of the mail van were three mail sorters, S. Scott, E. Bristol and H. Clark. They had finished sorting the mails and were busy tying the letters in bundles in the rear part of the coach when the crash came. Clark found he was jammed tightly between the wall of the van and a pile of wreckage, with no room to move. He was in pain and was dazed by the shock. The lights had gone out but he could hear the hiss of gas escaping from the reservoir under the seat.

Clark called to his two companions, who did not respond at first. When they did he found they were quite near him. The three men joined hands and, exerting their combined strength, extricated themselves, but only with great difficulty. They then crawled through masses of splintered wood, mail bags and debris to a hole in the side of the coach. Further progress was barred by the side of the telescoped sleeping car, which blocked their exit. The three postal employees then struggled

A semaphore signal in the off position, meaning that a train may pass.

along the narrow passage until they reached a window, through which they managed to escape. Passengers on the outside helped them to the ground.

Two trained nurses on the express train gave immediate first aid and, in due course, two doctors from Pukekohe arrived on the relief train.

Evidence at the inquest concentrated on the condition of the signal, set on the platform pull-over lever at danger, yet 550 m away showing green for all clear. The search for the truth was stimulated by the fact that this was the first accident on New Zealand railways due to a signal defect.

A semaphore signal consisted of an arm, which was pulled down or 'off' to indicate that a train may pass it, or the horizontal or 'on' position indicating a 'stop'. Fixed to the inner end of the arm was a frame containing red and green glasses, which moved with the arm before a lamp, so that at night red is shown for 'danger' and green for 'go-ahead' or 'all clear'. The frame holding the coloured glasses was roughly kidney shaped and the device was known as the spectacle; only a narrow strip of metal separated the colours. This red or green signal was not visible to the officer operating the signal. His only guide was the small, white back light.

At the inquest the driver of the express, John Stone, gave evidence that after the accident he walked back to the signal, which was showing green without any sign of red. The lever on the station platform he found to be locked and set at danger. Both the fireman and guard of the express also said that they had found the signal in this condition.

The guard, James Wilson, noticed the signal wire was very tight. This wire, 21 mm (7/8 in) thick steel, ran between the control lever on the station platform and the signal on pulleys attached to stakes alongside the line. Wilson considered the wire to be too tight to allow the signal to be put back to danger. Other witnesses put forward a theory that the tightness of the wire must have been due to its contraction in the cold weather, on this the coldest night of the year to date.

A 584, the locomotive involved in the Whangamarino accident, leaves Mercer with the Auckland to Wellington express.

This theory was dismissed when Henry Wynn, signalling and electrical engineer for the Railways Department, took the stand. He had never read of a case, he said, of a signal being pulled off to the 'clear' position by the contraction of the wire alone. He was more interested in evidence given by a signal adjuster, John Cruickshank who, six months before the accident, had placed a small wheel where a large one should have been used in the signal's control mechanism. It was through this that the wire ran on the signal gantry. In Henry Wynn's opinion, the failure of the signal was due to the wire being set too tight — the contraction of the wire would then be bound to pull the signal. Cruickshank had found it necessary to set the wire tighter than it should have been to get it to work over the small reel he had placed on the signal.

On the fateful morning, with the first really cold weather since the alterations were made by Cruickshank, the contraction of the already overtight wire gradually pulled the signal spectacle over until the full green light was shown, the controlling lever at the platform still remaining locked at the danger position. Wynn dismissed other possible causes of the accident. Having installed the electric train tablet system, he felt qualified to say that the system neither contributed to nor could have prevented the accident.

'There was a fortune,' he said, 'waiting for anyone who could invent a signalling system which was absolutely reliable. . . . The system of crossing trains, as at Whangamarino on the night of the accident, was in accordance with the best railway practice for single line systems.'[4]

In endeavouring to cross the trains, as he did, the tablet porter Donaldson was acting strictly in accordance with regulations. His only fault, from the railway point of view, was that he failed to see that his signal was properly at 'danger' by observing the back light.

So we come to the coroner's verdict. He found Cruickshank guilty of an honest error of judgement in a threefold breach of the regulations — in making alterations without instructions,

A semaphore signal in the on position, meaning 'stop'.

The point of collision, showing the intersection of lines over which the freight train was being shunted on to a station siding.

in putting in unsuitable material which did not conform to requirements and in failing to report in detail what he had done. This, however, did not amount to culpable negligence. The driver of the express train, John Stone, was exonerated from all blame and complimented for his presence of mind.

William Donaldson was labelled the culprit. In the coroner's opinion there was no excuse for the tablet porter's lack of vigilance. A signal might be pulled over by a cow fouling the wire, or even by some mischievous person tampering with it. Donaldson had last observed the back white light of the south signal at 12.10 a.m. on the morning of the tragedy, four and a half hours before the express was due. He had not bothered to check again, although he knew it was the only safeguard between the express and disaster. He was found guilty of culpable negligence in not checking the signal and as a result of this finding he was charged with the crime of manslaughter, of which he was subsequently acquitted.

The coroner paid tribute to the frankness and truthfulness of all witnesses, including the men implicated who 'made no attempt to shirk any blame'.[5] Also, in quoting evidence that in the nine years before the Whangamarino accident, no fewer than 123 million passengers had been carried on New Zealand railways without the loss of one life, he concluded: 'It is questionable if any other railway system in the world can point to such results.'[6]

Engine Wab 686 buried by the slip at Mataroa with the wrecked vans and telescoped first carriage. In the background is the relief train which brought doctors, nurses and equipment from Taihape. The suddenness of this substantial slip, which caught the Auckland to Wellington express in transit, is emphasised by the fact that another train had passed that way only half an hour before.

Mataroa 8 November 1918

The body of an engine driver, a victim of the influenza epidemic at Ohakune in 1918, was being conveyed south for interment when the train ploughed into a falling slip 2 km (1½ miles) north of Mataroa. As was usual, the mortuary van was immediately behind the engine and, in this instance, separated from the passenger carriages by a mail van.

When the engine ploughed into a large landslide of earth, trees and rocks, the mortuary van took the immediate shock; the coffin containing the body was thrown clear of the line without being in any way damaged. But the postal van was completely wrecked and the two postal officials working inside it were killed straightaway, and the first carriage telescoped the vans ahead.

But for the buffer offered by the mortuary van, passengers in the first carriage would have been exposed to much greater danger. As it was, one died instantly, another died of injuries and, in all, eight other passengers were sufficiently hurt to be taken to hospital. Others, including the slightly hurt, were able to resume their journey.

Again, the accident might have been much worse but for the fireman spotting the slip falling on to the line as the Auckland to Wellington express rounded a curve at a fair speed. He promptly called for brakes, which were immediately applied by the driver, but too late to avoid dashing into the falling slip.

Many, including women and children, were extricated unhurt. One woman was found by the rescue gang sitting in an overturned carriage nursing a child. Both were rescued through a window. A male passenger was trapped in wreckage for more than three hours, while others told of hair's-breadth escapes.

Even while uninjured passengers were attending those who had been hurt, the cry was raised, 'Another slip is coming down.' And suddenly down it came, bringing more of the hillside with it. Trees and huge papa rocks fell and buried the engine, Wab 686. The locality of the slip had not been regarded as dangerous, but the slip began well back from the railway line.

The locomotive of the Auckland–Wellington express almost wholly buried in the landslide across the line at Mataroa. The engine did not plough in as deeply as this but was caught in a second slip.

A picture taken soon after daybreak not long after the Auckland–Wellington express ploughed into a landslide across the line near Ongarue, with tragic loss of life. Behind the wrecked engine, still steaming, are the derailed tender and postal van and the telescoped carriages in which 17 passengers were killed or died of injuries.

Ongarue 6 July 1923

The first major loss of life on New Zealand railways happened on 6 July 1923, 0.75 km (half a mile) south of Ongarue, on the North Island Main Trunk. A sudden landslide round a blind corner derailed the southbound Auckland to Wellington express, killing 17 passengers and injuring 28. Both the driver and fireman were also severely scalded.

Disaster struck a few minutes before 6 o'clock on a cold frosty morning. Although it was still dark, there was good visibility from the locomotive's powerful headlight as the train drifted down a slight incline with steam shut off. A massive landslip across the line ahead was hidden by high banks at a sharp bend. Driver Alec Stewart applied the full power of the brakes when he first saw the slip, only 2 or 3 m (6–10ft) ahead, but before the brakes could respond the engine ploughed into a mountain of slushy mud and rubble.

Between the rails and embedded in the slip was a boulder 1.25 m (4 ft) in diameter and weighing more than a tonne. But for this obstruction the engine might have pushed its way through the debris to safety. Instead, the boulder was carried for about 40 m (2 chains) on the cowcatcher until its great weight flung the locomotive, tender and postal van, with a violent lurch, off the rails and against the bank of the cutting.

Passengers comfortable in the sleeping cars towards the end of the train felt next to nothing and most slept on until awoken so that their bunk sheets could be taken for bandages. But up

One of the telescoped carriages after being pulled apart at the scene of the disaster. Little of the interior remained intact.

forward, all was chaos. At least 12 passengers were killed in the moment of catastrophe, which left the engine's whistle blowing at full blast and steam hissing in clouds from the safety valves and rising high into the grey light of the dawn. Added to this was the full glare of the fires, exposed when the door of the firebox had been wrenched off.

When the engine, tender and postal van toppled over, they were removed from the danger of being telescoped. Farther back on the curve the first of the second-class carriages stood as a buffer and the two coaches following it at almost 50 km (30 miles) an hour came on and inflicted the direct shock, not only upon the car in front but also on each other.

The second carriage, a second-class smoker, was driven right through the first with terrific force, only 0.5 m (2 ft) separating the front doors of both carriages. One side of the first carriage was smashed to fragments, while there was no sign of the roof except for thousands of splinters spread everywhere. So great was the impact that the rear wheels of the second carriage were driven through on to the floor of the first carriage. The second carriage suffered the most damage. The following car ran up on top of the second carriage, the three being telescoped. The cars behind these three were sufficiently around the curve to be just out of line of direct shock and escaped with a shaking and some broken windows.

First to suffer were the engine driver, Alec Stewart, and his fireman, Bill Campbell, who were immediately blasted with steam escaping from the broken steam injector. One end of the pipe was turned towards the fireman, trapped between the engine and the cutting bank. In trying to rescue him, the driver was severely burnt on one arm, adding to the bruises to the head and body he had suffered in the crash. A passenger helped the driver extricate Campbell who, however, was left to stagger in intense pain alongside the track, until he collapsed, still calling for help.

Guard H. P. Hobson, in his brake van at the rear of the train, felt three distinct phases of the stoppage — 'the first impression of striking a slip and a sudden stop, the second that of something settling and the third the dead stop.'

Almost immediately one of the gas containers under the third carriage burst into flames and it looked as if the whole train would be enveloped by the blaze. A passenger jumped down to where the flames were erupting and began to heap mud on to the outbreak, but his efforts were successfully dwarfed by another slip which smothered the gas, preventing the fire from spreading.

The worst casualties were in the carriage immediately behind the postal van, where three postal officers had escaped with a few scratches because of the very strong construction of their vehicle. The first carriage was carrying from 25 to 30 passengers, the second carriage was full and the third car carried seven or eight people. All three had been welded together and those passengers who survived were in a dreadful plight. To get them out the roof of the first carriage had to be cut open.

Several survivors who had seen service in France in the First World War compared the scene with the battlefield. Wilfred Cribb recalled how he had been 'in some tight corners on the other side of the world but never so tight a corner as this'.[1] He noted how many imprisoned passengers suffered from the fumes of escaping gas, which blackened their faces. One young returned man, spiked through the chest, declined a drink of brandy, saying, 'No, give it to the others, they need it more than me. I'm about all in.'[2] He died before reaching Taumarunui. Another injured man, given a hot drink, said 'God bless you, old man', and fell back dead.[3]

C. George, of Wellington, was asleep in the front of the third carriage, covered by his rug and with his feet up on the seat opposite, when 'the accident happened in one tremendous shock and it was all over. . . . The floor and ceiling of [the second] car, which was practically wiped out of existence, were driven in upon us, cutting their way through the carriage like a knife through cheese, smashing the seats before them as they came. We were all flung up towards the ceiling.'[4]

He spent some 20 minutes among the debris, in darkness, not knowing where he and his trapped companions were or what would happen next. Then guard Hobson hailed them from outside before beginning to attack the side of the carriage with a hammer and saw, but it took a relief gang to free the imprisoned and one by one the passengers were lifted out to safety.

H. P. Hobson, guard on the wrecked train, by the window which he broke with his hand to go to the rescue. Mrs Donald, who was killed, occupied the seat marked X.

Wreckage of a second-class carriage awaiting attention from the breakdown gang. The men lit splintered wreckage for illumination and warmth.

The skeleton of one of the telescoped carriages being removed.

The locomotive Ab 748 and the driver, Alec Stewart, photographed by W. W. Stewart before the accident.

An acknowledged hero of the rescue efforts was A. H. Croucher, of Christchurch, who was able to take initiatives because he had a torch. In the far end of the third carriage, he was washing in the toilet compartment when the crash happened and was pushed tight against a partition. Suddenly the pressure ceased — a few millimetres more and he would have been crushed to death.

He was released in time to escort people to safety, then returned to see what more he could do. A Seventh Day Adventist, he became firmly convinced he owed his life to the interposition of providence. 'I am glad,' he said, 'that at the moment of the crash I had the hymn on my lips, "God will take care of me".'[5]

Four or five women in the third carriage kept calling, 'Look out for the children.'[6] Some men got out of the next compartment, which was undamaged, and helped the injured. A child who was bleeding and had both legs broken was passed out. As he was laid down gently, he said, 'Mummy will be here soon.'[7]

One woman was sitting upright, dead, with a look of calmness on her face, but her body was frightfully crushed. A young woman had an arm projecting through the window and one foot protruding through a hole in the side of the carriage. She was appealing for help.

Guard Hobson saw 'many heart-rending sights' as he moved from one part of the train to another in his anxiety to do the utmost possible for the injured. 'At one time,' he recalled, 'I would be on the roof of a car, at another in the train and again on the top of the bank helping to drag the dead and maimed out through windows or through gaps we had cut in the tops and sides of the car.'[8]

He was one of many who did their best until professional help arrived from Ongarue and Taumarunui and in the meantime he prayed for daylight. The only illumination early in the rescue work came from the guard's flashlight and three electric torches owned by passengers.

Uninjured and some lightly injured passengers went to work with a will, helping two fellow passengers — Dr D. A. Bathgate, of Turua, Hauraki Plains, and H. H. Nash, a medical student — to the point where an observer reported: 'Now the dead, dying and injured were being released expeditiously and carried to the side of the track, where they were placed on cushions and covered with blankets supplied by the passengers. Their injuries were ministered to. It was bitterly cold with a hard frost.'[9]

In addition to blankets, rugs and cushions, flasks of hot drinks (coffee mainly) and whisky and brandy were also supplied by helpful passengers. A messenger sent by guard Hobson alerted the Ongarue tablet porter to the disaster and he roused permanent way staff living near the station and the first helpers left for the accident with axes, saws and stretchers while their wives lit fires and prepared to receive victims.

No one took charge of Ongarue's arrangements to help those in distress. Everyone mobilised the resources available and every woman in the town was soon ready with appliances and comforts, so that from the time the alarm was given till the last of the injured passengers had left for Taumarunui, residents worked unremittingly. As one woman later remarked, 'Not a tap of housework was done in Ongarue that day,' all effort being concentrated on the accident survivors.[10]

The house nearest the scene of the accident, occupied by A. H. Levein, a ganger on the railway, was transformed into a temporary hospital and women helpers there, including a nurse who had served in the war, washed and bandaged as best they could. They noticed that a great number of patients had head injuries. The work of tending the injured at the scene of the accident was completed at last. A special train took them to Taumarunui where they were met by nurses and residents with cars and stretchers and conveyed to the hospital. Three died on the way.

Such was the response at Taumarunui to a call for volunteer helpers that many, including trained nurses, had to be turned away. The injured were transferred from the train to the hospital by car, in a slow-moving procession through the town, each serious case carried on a stretcher resting on the seats of the car and watched over by an attendant. The fortunate were able to make their way to Taumarunui unaided. Some did not want to stop long to count their blessings and became impatient when the Railways Department did not move them on their interrupted journey promptly, a fault subsequently ascribed to more slips waiting to be cleared.

Individuals had their own tales to tell, some of miraculous escapes. Members of a Maori rugby team had been accommodated in a specially reserved carriage at the front of the train,

Mrs W. Donald, of Auckland, the only woman passenger killed.

next to the mail van, the first carriage. Five minutes before departure time a Railway official made the team transfer to a first-class carriage in the middle of the train. Amid protests and grumbles the team bustled out with its luggage to the other car farther back, little dreaming their lives would be saved by this action. A woman and her baby found her seat double-booked, so moved back into another car. An elderly man who was in the seat was killed.

Members of the Scandal Theatrical Company found their reserved car was not in its allotted place when they joined the train at Te Awamutu; it should have been at the front of the train. In the right-hand corner of the first car four men had been playing cards when the impact came. Miraculously they escaped injury.

No one could have foreseen the landslip. The area had never previously given trouble and had been patrolled and inspected shortly before the accident. Reassurance that tracks were in fact patrolled conscientiously was printed in the wake of the disaster: '. . . every yard of the Main Trunk is inspected early every morning, including Sundays, by surfacemen, either on jiggers or on foot. Each surfaceman has from three miles upwards to watch, but the average is about six miles for each man. . . . The men engaged are all men of experience.'[11]

A board of inquiry exonerated the Railways Department from any suggestion of negligence over this Ongarue disaster. Clearly it had resulted from causes — excessive rain — over which the Department had no control.

Notwithstanding that the Railways Department was under no legal liability to pay any compensation to passengers, assistance was given those 'in a position of necessity' as the result of the accident.

Of various suggestions made by the board of inquiry, it was agreed that cars used for Main Trunk express traffic should be specially strengthened to reduce the possibility of telescoping. Guards' vans' ambulance and tools equipment was increased, after trenchant criticism of inadequate supplies made by Dr Bathgate at the inquest.

Although it had been decided to equip Main Trunk express trains throughout with electric light, the work was now given priority. As the department's annual report noted, 'This work . . . when complete, will not only provide a more efficient and satisfactory light and increase the comfort of passengers, but will also reduce the danger of fire occurring in the case of serious accidents.'[12]

The last word on this 1923 tragedy at Ongarue can be left with Dr Bathgate. He was the only doctor on the train and he stayed on at Taumarunui for two days to help at the hospital. Impressed with the local response, he was to write: 'The Taumarunui doctors and staff rose nobly to the sudden influx of dead, dying and injured patients. In such conditions you see your fellow citizens at their best.'[13]

The burnt-out wreck of the Wellington to Napier mail train which left the rails at high speed near Opapa in September 1925. The locomotive was A 600, and had been driven by the Prince of Wales, later the Duke of Windsor, during his visit to New Zealand in 1920.

Opapa 22 September 1925

Wellington merchant Arthur Allen had suffered a great deal from shock after surviving the 1923 Ongarue rail disaster, so much so that he had not ridden on a train until now, two years later. On 22 September 1925 he caught the Wellington to Napier mail train to visit Hawke's Bay. Little did he realise that he was riding to his second rail disaster.

All should have gone well. The wheels and running gear of the locomotive, which had taken the express from Napier to Woodville earlier in the day, had been inspected by the locomotive foreman at Napier. The track had been checked that morning and the usual weekly inspection had also been made. And while the train was at Waipukurau, on the run north, the Westinghouse brake system had been tested and the wheels and undergear of the vehicles examined and found to be in good order. All that could be at possible risk was the human factor.

Although obviously mindful of his Ongarue experience, Arthur Allen would have enjoyed the journey. This was a latent memory, until the train entered the first sweep of an S bend on the track about 1.5 km (1 mile) south of Opapa, a little Maori settlement 43 km (27 miles) south of Napier and lying a little north of Te Aute College, the famous school for Maori youth. The carriage in which Arthur Allen sat gave an alarming lurch, so pronounced that he braced himself against the seat in front of him, while a distressing mental picture arose of what he had gone through at Ongarue.

At the next bend the lurch was even more sudden, bringing items tumbling down from the carriage luggage racks. Then the carriage suddenly tilted up, the wheels on one side having left the track. Immediately there was a sudden jolting, though it was not very severely felt in Arthur Allen's carriage. He was standing now, having jumped to his feet when the wheels lifted. He scrambled out, to a scene of twisted steel, splintered wood and broken glass. The engine and six of the nine carriages had been derailed on the 150 m (7½ chain) curve while descending a grade of 1 in 46 between the top of the grade siding and Opapa station. The engine took the first carriage, a second-class smoker, with it and threw it on its side, where the top of the cutting fell away to a comparatively low bank.

This carriage suffered the most severe damage and its occupants were the most seriously injured. The forward compartment had smashed into the engine tender and the back end had been shorn off by the other cars as they had careered past. Although the floor was intact, the sides and ceiling were in splinters and broken panelling sagged above the wreckage of seats and fittings.

The coupling between the first and second carriages snapped cleanly, allowing the remaining carriages to go madly forward downhill and so evade telescoping on the front of the train. These carriages did not travel more than a few metres past the engine until they, too, left the rails and crashed into the right side of the cutting. Some part of the wrecked engine caught the front carriage and ripped its side out cleanly along its entire length, taking the single seats out of the first-class compartment.

The last man brought out from the carriage coupled to the engine was unhurt. He had been buried at the extreme end of the car, next to the tender. Another, imprisoned on his feet by wreckage, was bleeding freely from a wound on his face. But he was relatively lucky, for a piece of sharp timber had penetrated his clothing though it had not broken the skin. Had it gone another few millimetres, it would have killed him.

Beneath the upturned wheels of a carriage, huddled on the shingle of the track, was Miss Kathleen Begley, of Hastings. Both her legs had been almost severed. She died in Hastings Hospital. She was returning from Waipukurau, where she had been to the wedding of her brother, and was to have been married herself in a week.

The other passenger to die, E. V. Iggulden, of Wairoa, was in one of the carriages which had run on past the engine. One of his arms had been almost wrenched off, a leg had been broken and he had suffered head injuries. He was conscious when found by Nurse H. Badger on a seat in a carriage with the side torn out, and although fearfully injured, he had handed over his papers, to be kept.

In the carriages which had run past the engine, several passengers sitting on the left-hand side were badly injured, particularly about the legs. The fireman was thrown through the cab window, the engine driver was badly scalded.

Survivors plunged into the wreckage to retrieve the injured, working against time and a fire which spread quickly. 'Remi-

One of the wrecked carriages after the fire, with only the seat supports standing. The locomotive is in the background.

niscent of a battlefield,' wrote a Napier reporter who travelled by the relief train to the Opapa scene. 'Scattered about the fields which basked in summer sunshine and beautiful in their freshness and greenness lay the injured people, little knots of helpers hastening here and there to their aid and doing a hundred kindnesses to allay their suffering. The hillside was graphically reminiscent of a battlefield and the injured with their bandaged limbs, some of them being borne on the crudest of stretchers to a collecting point, gave a sad appearance to the otherwise purely pastoral scene.'[1]

Emergency operations were carried out by a doctor who travelled on the wrecked train and by Nurse Badger. While a Napier businessman held the limb, the doctor amputated one of Miss Begley's terribly injured legs — with a penknife. With another penknife, Nurse Badger amputated E. V. Iggulden's arm, which had been almost severed. Splints and bandages carried in the guard's van were woefully inadequate. Splints were improvised from broken timbers and railway towels. Women's torn-up linen was used as bandages.

What impressed A. E. Renouf of Napier, during the rescue work, was the heroic attitude of injured passengers as they were helped out of the wrecked carriages. Some were severely injured, but all seemed more concerned about others than themselves. Most said: 'I'm all right. How are the others?'[2]

In the meantime, carriages began to burn fiercely, sending up great clouds of smoke. The engine, in leaving the track, had scattered dead and burning coal over the track and on nearby pasture, igniting the Pintsch gas liberated in the carriages by the rupture of the cylinders and their connections. Five carriages were completely destroyed by fire.

On a count taken just after 5 p.m., 50 minutes after the accident, about 150 motor vehicles had come from all parts of the district, attracted by the billowing smoke. Their owners put themselves completely at the disposal of distressed passengers.

A commission of inquiry was appointed on 23 September 1925, but it adjourned its hearings until the completion of charges against the engine driver. He was duly convicted of the crime of manslaughter and sentenced in the Napier Supreme Court. The jury found that he had failed to exercise reasonable care and skill in driving the engine before and at the time of the derailment and that excessive speed was the primary cause of the derailment.

The three-man commission agreed with this verdict, finding that the train had been travelling at the rate of at least 65 km (40 miles) an hour while descending the Opapa grade at a point where the speed was limited to 40 km (25 miles) an hour. Speed boards indicating the radius of each curve were in their proper position. The driver had therefore been guilty of excessive speed when approaching the curves near which the derailment took place, thus causing the derailment.

The commission also found that the presence of a third person on the engine, and the taking of liquor on to the engine by that person, were factors in the derailment.

The mail train was hauled by steam Pacific class locomotive A 600 and had been driven by the Prince of Wales (later the Duke of Windsor) during his visit to New Zealand in 1920.

Ratana 26 March 1938. The projecting side of the first carriage (left) which capsized with the engine, tore through the sides of the remaining carriages as they ran past on the right.

The wrecked excursion train near Ratana, which came to grief when locomotive Ab 829 took a curve at excessive speed and capsized. As a result seven people were killed and 40 injured.

Ratana 26 March 1938

Easter in the later 1930s was not only a time for religious thanksgiving but also an opportunity to celebrate school jubilee reunions, sporting occasions and railway excursions, such as that which left Wellington at 9.45 p.m. on Good Friday 1938 for destinations north to New Plymouth. The train consisted of six passenger cars and a guard's van, pulled by locomotive Ab 829. Most passengers were visiting friends and relatives in Wanganui and New Plymouth especially, a practice observed in many other parts of the country as people took advantage of the long holiday weekend.

Engine driver Edward Percival had not driven over the section of line between Marton and Wanganui for about eight years, but had no hesitation in accepting the assignment for train W4. He was confident his knowledge of the track was sufficient, based on four previous night trips between Wellington and New Plymouth.

Experienced drivers were to support him on this matter, agreeing that when a driver had driven over a section of track on a few occasions he was able to remember that section for an indefinite number of years thereafter. Department policy was to permit a driver to decline an assignment if he considered he was insufficiently familiar with the section of line over which the train was to run; it was not held against him in any way if he declined the assignment for that reason. Driver Percival had no qualms.

Yet he overlooked one vital factor which was to help confuse memory and was to bring death, injury, distress and damage to passengers and rolling stock — early morning haze and banks of fog.

Would greater familiarity with the track have made the engine driver more cautious when, just after 2 a.m. on 26 March 1938, he ran into fog at a position he estimated to be just under a kilometre (½ mile) beyond Ratana but which, in fact, was about 1.2 km (¾ mile) beyond that station? It was a fatal error.

At the time he was looking for a speed restriction board near a 130 m (6.4 chain) radius curve but he did not expect to see it until he had proceeded another 360 m (50 chains). Indeed, he did not see the speed board at all, because of the bank of fog which reduced visibility to a distance of about 20 m (1 chain), and possibly also because he had turned his head to give an instruction to his fireman.

The driver made a short, light application of the brakes when he thought he was about 600 m (30 chains) from the curve but it was not enough to effect a substantial reduction of speed. At that time the engine was within 60 m (200 ft) of the point of derailment, which happened almost immediately after the brakes had been released.

The cause of the derailment, said the subsequent board of inquiry, 'was the overturning of the engine, due to it entering a curve of 130 metre radius at a speed of about 80 km (50 miles) an hour,'[1] at a point 6.5 km (4 miles) north of Turakina on the Ratana flat. The maximum speed limit on the section of line was 55 km (35 miles) an hour, with a special speed restriction at the accident scene of 32 km (20 miles) an hour.

On leaving the rails the engine, tender and leading car fell outwards to the left against the side of the cutting and travelled over the sleepers and ballast and along the cess (batter) for more than 40 m (142 ft). The cab was twisted and torn out of shape, the tender was partly telescoped into the cab and the cowcatcher and front bogies were buried into the clay bank.

The couplings and brake hose between the first and second cars parted and the second, third and fourth cars continued on the curve until they struck the right-hand corner of the derailed and tilted leading car, causing them to be thrown off the rails to the right. The leading bogie of the fifth car was also derailed to the right, leaving firm on the rails the sixth car and the guard's van.

The leading end of the second car travelled more than 35 m (121 ft) beyond the point of derailment or 90 m (304 ft) from its position where the engine left the rails. The fourth carriage came to a halt alongside the derailed locomotive and in the 600 mm gap (2 ft) between the two vehicles two bodies and two fatally injured passengers were found. It was remarkable that the first carriage escaped with comparatively little structural damage, but the next three cars were turned into masses of debris.

Six passengers died as the result of the accident, more than

40 people were treated for injuries and 13 were admitted to Wanganui Hospital. Among those admitted were the driver and his fireman, both with severe burns, the former in a condition described as 'fair', the latter as 'critical'. Both were trapped in the cab, with scalding steam enveloping them and fireman Ken Miller eventually died in hospital, to make seven deaths.

As usual, survivors turned to rescue work, though hampered by the pitch black early morning darkness and lack of medical materials. Among the rescue squad, quickly on the scene from Palmerston North, was a hospital staff member who found 'one of the most ghastly scenes' he had ever witnessed — and he had gone through the First World War.[2]

Members of the board of inquiry showed sympathy for the driver:

> He was a steady, competent, experienced driver with a first-class record. They did not consider him guilty of culpable negligence, but were of the opinion that although he admitted travelling over the Ratana flat at a speed that he himself estimated to be five miles an hour in excess of the maximised authorised speed, his miscalculation of his speed and location was due to an honest error of judgement, to which the presence of haze and fog contributed. His failure to reduce speed considerably, as a measure of prudence when the train ran into fog, is attributable to the same error of judgement.[3]

Although the driver should not have driven over the Ratana flat at a speed in excess of 55 km (35 m) an hour, his considered speed of 65 km (40 miles) an hour would not in fact have been a dangerous speed.

Another view of the derailed train near Ratana.

The report recommended that speed recorders be installed on all engines used for hauling express, mail and passenger trains. The inability to judge speed was primarily the cause of the derailment. The board added:

> . . . in everyday practice trains must frequently operate under conditions prejudicial to any rapid and accurate judgement of speed, such as the strict observance of restrictions over difficult sections necessarily demands. It is certainly over to question whether even the most experienced men can judge their instantaneous train-speed with any approach to accuracy under unfavourable conditions, for example, storm or fog. We incline to the view also that the expectation of accuracy of judgement within a margin of two miles per hour either way is too optimistic for general acceptation, even under fairly good conditions and in daylight.[4]

Throughout the night rescue workers at Hyde continued the search for victims and survivors, slowly clearing the giant heap of rubble, all that remained of the leading carriages. The locomotive was Ab 782.

Hyde 4 June 1943

'It is safe to say that no previous railway accident in this country has resulted in such a mass of distorted and wrecked rolling stock.' So said the board of inquiry appointed to report on one of the most disastrous accidents to have happened on the New Zealand railways until that time.

Twenty-one passengers were killed and 47 people were injured when the engine of the Cromwell to Dunedin express left the rails at 1.45 p.m. on 4 June 1943 and crashed on to its side while rounding a curve in a deep cutting south of Hyde on the Central Otago line. There were 113 passengers on the train, many bound for the Winter Show in Dunedin and for the races at Wingatui.

Forewarning of the disaster could have been read in the excessive speed at which the train was travelling, sufficient to throw luggage and parcels from the racks and to cause the cars to sway to an alarming extent.

'Minutes before the accident the passengers were falling about the carriage because of the way in which it was swaying,' said Philip Banon, of Dunedin.[1] His carriage, the second from the engine, overturned a full length ahead of where the engine had come to rest 60 m (200 ft) ahead of the point of derailment. Fortunately Banon escaped injury and other passengers were to pay tribute to his 'magnificent' efforts helping to direct rescue work and aiding the injured.

All seven carriages were derailed and four of them telescoped when locomotive Ab 782 left the rails soon after it had entered a curve of almost 200 m (10 chains) radius.

The impact was such that one man, of medium build, was thrown right out a carriage window. As the carriage hurtled over he struck the bank of the cutting and boomeranged back through another window. He suffered superficial cuts. Also

A night view at Hyde from the rear of the express as the search continued for victims. The first-class cars at the rear (pictured) had their leading ends telescoped and the cars were thrown askew the track but passengers largely escaped injury.

fortunate was Mrs Mavis Sawera, of Alexandra, who just before the crash had given up her seat to a woman with a baby in her arms and moved to a corner seat. The mother and child were killed. But Mrs Sawera was trapped in the torn and twisted wreckage for more than six hours, with a fractured leg and severe shock.

A farmer who heard, then saw the crash, ran 1.5 km (1 mile) to telephone for help, and returned to find his son's mangled body. The youth had been returning to Army camp after leave. Another passenger, an elderly woman, survived, but lost her husband, a daughter and two grandchildren in the disaster.

Because of difficulties in communication it was about one and a half hours before rescuers began to arrive. In the meantime passengers from the rear carriages tended the injured — where they could be reached in the great tangled mass of steel and wood, with carriage heaped upon carriage.

Evidence produced for the board of inquiry included the startling fact that an underframe of one of the carriages had been twisted into the form of a letter S, indicating an impact of such tremendous force that it was not likely to have been possible at a speed of less than 112 km (70 miles) an hour. Regulations required the train to pass the point of derailment at a limit of 48 km (30 miles) an hour.

The inquiry found that the cause of derailment was the overturning of the engine through the operation of centrifugal force, resulting from the engine entering a curve of 183 m (9.88 chains) radius at excessive speed. Further, the board found the engine driver guilty of serious dereliction of duty and that the 'reckless manner' in which he drove his engine was the cause of the derailment. The guard had his wrist slapped for not taking counter-action when the train's speed became excessive.

Evidence convinced the board that the engine driver had 'taken a quantity of alcohol sufficient to affect his judgement and sense of responsibility and to a marked degree, and that during the journey he took more alcohol'; he had carried some bottles of beer on the engine.[2]

He was charged in the Dunedin Supreme Court with manslaughter, having killed certain persons 'by driving a railway train negligently and at excessive speed'.[3] He was found guilty and sentenced to three years' reformative detention. Regulations relating to alcohol and drugs in the service were tightened to try and ensure that nothing like this would happen again.

After the inquiry a man pulled to safety from the wreckage and taken to Dunedin was killed that night, crossing a road. The board of inquiry's verdict made the Minister of Railways, the Hon. R. Semple, liable for compensation claims. About $400,000 was paid out.

Suspicions were often raised in railway accident inquiries about alcohol having affected the crew's performance, and almost always the crews were completely cleared. The Hyde tragedy was an unhappy exception.

Haywards 8 November 1943

Thirty Wab engines were in service in New Zealand when a spectacular accident on the Hutt line near Haywards, 24 km (15 miles) from Wellington, involving Wab 794, brought a query about the practice of running these engines bunker first on other than a high standard permanent way.

Designed to run at full service speeds in either direction (which a tender engine could not do safely), the Wab was then the heaviest locomotive in service except the K. When running bunker first, the leading pair of wheels (the trailing wheels when running forward) were more heavily loaded than the leading wheels of any other engine then in use on the New Zealand Railways. All this came in for urgent consideration when a board of inquiry sat on an accident near Haywards on 8 November 1943.

Train No. 767, consisting of seven passenger cars and a van, left Upper Hutt station for Wellington at 7.25 a.m., hauled by locomotive Wab 794, running bunker first. There were about 300 passengers. Between Haywards and Andrews, about 7.50 a.m., the train was derailed, the engine running off the track with carriage piled upon carriage. The Wab engine ran a considerable distance in a partly derailed condition, until about 60 m (205 ft) from the point of derailment it was completely derailed, falling on its side against a bank.

Hard up against its front buffers was all that remained of the first carriage, an old 'straight-seater', with a guard's van compartment in the front. This carriage, except for a few splintered timbers at one end, was levelled to the floorboards. The carriage behind ran partially over it, tearing the whole bodywork away as it passed and came to a stop on the other side of the line. The following three carriages were left lying on their sides, crushed end to end and leaning over towards the river, giving the whole train a partially folded appearance.

Mrs N. P. Rowe — killed.

The front carriage was full of passengers and it seemed incredible that anyone could have escaped from this section of the train, yet this actually happened. One lucky man found himself walking in the open air just after the accident; he had stepped off what little remained of the carriage on to the roadway.

Some other passengers were not so lucky. Two young women were killed instantly, one man died of his injuries and 20 others, including the guard, were injured. Medical aid was quickly on the scene, although the first to arrive was a contingent of United States Marine Corps engineers. Then came doctors, nurses and orderlies with full field equipment from a United States naval hospital. They were soon joined by local doctors and medical staff from Trentham Camp.

Miss E. Ryrie — killed.

Two leg amputations were performed under emergency conditions at the site by the senior American medical officer, Surgeon Commander O. R. Myers, assisted by a New Zealand Army doctor. They worked in cramped conditions amid and

Two views of the damaged carriages at Haywards. That on the right shows the completely demolished first carriage.

under wreckage. At one time the American surgeon remained under the wreckage with an injured man while railway breakdown workers tried to remove the wreckage pinning him down. Two nurses also stood by the trapped patients, while blood transfusions were given by American personnel using field plasma equipment.

The two young women who were killed and the two passengers whose legs were amputated before they could be extricated were jammed close together in the wreckage where they had been swept under the dislodged rear bogie of the second carriage, practically under the point where it was telescoped with the third carriage.

An oxy-acetylene plant was brought from Trentham and used to try to free a middle-aged man pinned by twisted ironwork. One iron bar was cut through but the task of releasing him without the need for amputating his leg was hopeless. Operating equipment was placed on the bare floor of the smashed carriage alongside and the operation performed. He died later in hospital. Several passengers were admitted to the United States naval hospital and others had outpatient treatment there and at Wellington Public Hospital.

The Railways Department's travelling 40 tonne crane arrived at midday to clear the permanent way and a US Marine squad also arrived with a heavy road crane to help lift the wreckage so that the dead could be extricated.

The Wab engine, running in reverse (a practice common on suburban lines), had begun to leave the line about a rail's length before reaching the point where reballasting and resleepering had taken place. The smash happened on this section. Beyond the point of derailment the whole section of line over which the train had passed after leaving the rails had moved more than 150 mm (6 ins) to the left under the influence of the wheels running inside the track. The permanent way between the point of the derailment and where the engine fell over on its side was in a bad state after the accident for a distance of about 140 m (several chains).

Both engine and track came under searching investigation by the board of inquiry and defects in the track were found to be the primary cause of the accident. Sharp variations in cant (a term used to signify elevation of the outer rail above the inner rail on a curve) and extensive wear of the rails were blamed.

The board reported: 'We are not prepared to say definitely whether or not the variations in cant originated wholly or partly within a few days or a few hours before the time of derailment, but we are convinced that they were there immediately before the accident occurred and that they, together with the side wear of the head of the outer rail, were the primary cause of the derailment.'

The board quoted with approval an English report on the causes of derailment and the performances of locomotives, as measured in India:

> It is axiomatic that no track can be so perfectly designed and maintained that it will not contain some irregularities, however minute;

> and similarly no engine can be so perfectly designed that it will not respond in some measure to these irregularities. Apart from mere physical imperfections, it must be borne in mind that permanent-way is, by its very nature, an elastic structure which can never be completely unyielding. The difference between good and bad track is, therefore, one of degree, and any vehicle which is intended to run thereon must be so designed that the effect of track imperfections on its stability is reduced to a minimum.[1]

Accordingly, it seemed certain to the board of inquiry that the Wab engine, travelling bunker first, could not and did not respond to the irregularities in the track.

It was disquieting, therefore, to find that against large increases 'in train-miles, train-loads and gross ton-miles' on the Hutt Valley section (of the Railways) from 1938–39 to 1942–43,[2] there had been a marked decrease in the effective manpower of line gangs, not only in hours worked but in the quality of workers because of manpower demands of the Armed Forces.

While recognising any restriction on the free use of Wab engines must add to the difficulties of the transportation branch of the department in handling the heavy suburban traffic on the Wellington to Upper Hutt section, the board still found 'it necessary to recommend that Wab engines in this service should not be run bunker first until the chief engineer is satisfied that the permanent way has been adequately strengthened and that he is able to maintain it at a standard sufficiently high for the safe running of this class of engine bunker first.'[3]

Oddly enough this derailment happened only 150 mm (6 ft) north of the point where a train running to the same time schedule had left the line three months previously. By an even greater coincidence the train had been drawn by the same Wab locomotive. The first accident had been due to the failure of the centre casting of the leading bogie on the engine.

This photograph shows clearly the destroyed second carriage of the Picton–Christchurch express wrecked near Seddon.

Seddon 25 February 1948

Authorities differed on a matter of fact when they came to review the cause of the accident which wrecked the Picton to Christchurch express on 25 February 1948 between Blind River and Seddon about 30 km (19 miles) south of Blenheim. Six people died and 63 were injured, including the driver and fireman.

The immediate cause of the accident was unchallenged — the overturning first of the tender, then the engine (Ab 696), after entering a curve of 170 m (8.4 chains) at more than 80 km (52 miles) an hour. This was an excessive speed, to which engine driver Joseph William Gurr subsequently admitted to having been 'over confident'. As to entering the curve at the speed he did, he frankly admitted having made 'a terrific error'.[1]

But where did the fault lie? With the engine driver who, with less than 18 months' experience as an acting driver and on his first assignment driving an express train, was yet expected to keep the train to a tight schedule? And on a track with which, as a driver, he was relatively unfamiliar?

A board of inquiry into the accident found Gurr guilty of 'a serious dereliction of duty in driving the engine at a speed far in excess of that prescribed . . . [Gurr] can offer no explanation for the accident, but we are bound to say we are unable to understand how a driver with his experience and good record could fail to observe well-known regulations and neglect to exercise ordinary vigilance and judgement within sight of clearly defined and easily observed warning aids.'[2]

The board further found that the actions and decisions of the locomotive foreman at Christchurch and the senior driver at Kaikoura (in appointing acting driver Gurr to the run) were justified on the facts available. Yet when fireman and acting engine driver Gurr was charged with manslaughter in the

Ab 696 lying on its side between the bank of the cutting and the wreckage of the overtaking carriages. The locomotive capsized at a speed exceeding 84 km (52 miles) an hour on a 186 m (8.4 chain) curve.

Blenheim Supreme Court, the jury not only found him not guilty of the crime but added a rider to say that the cause of the disaster was 'the result of the inefficient administration of the Railways Department'.[3] Where did the truth lie?

Officers responsible for administering the Picton to Kaikoura line had their own problems, chief of which was recruiting first-grade engine drivers. When a replacement had to be found for the Kaikoura terminal, after a man had had to leave there, five Christchurch drivers were interviewed. All declined to go, for domestic reasons. 'Lack of housing and other amenities at country depots were substantially responsible for a general disinclination to accept appointments there,' the board of inquiry found.[4]

At the same inquiry, the district mechanical engineer at Christchurch, James Binstead, admitted it was usual to put special grade drivers, men who had had 24 years' experience, on the Christchurch to Invercargill express, but circumstances had contrived to the appointment of a first-year driver on the Picton to Christchurch express because of the difficulty of getting men to go to places such as Kaikoura. Express driving was not necessarily a prerogative of all first-class drivers, he said. Railways had first-class drivers they would not put on express trains, though the running of regular express trains was normally allotted to first-grade drivers.

James Binstead continued:

> Express passenger work carries higher prestige, particularly in the eyes of the public, and it is looked upon by the staff as a more congenial class of work. In general, they have better engines, cleaner work and less running interruptions than on goods trains and their home arrivals are more regular. Nevertheless, as far as knowledge of operating rules and mechanical knowledge is concerned, the men with the second-grade certificate, whether acting engine driver or engine driver, has the necessary knowledge to enable him to run any train with safety.
>
> Out of 702 trips of the expresses . . . operated by Kaikoura engine crews since December 1945, when the line opened, 508 were run by acting drivers.[5]

Binstead defended Gurr's transfer. Before this, Gurr had 'driven trains of heavy tonnage with our most powerful engine, the Kb class, over one of the most severe testing grounds for an engine driver that will be found anywhere in the Dominion, namely, between Springfield and Arthur's Pass. These trains are much heavier and accordingly more difficult to control than a passenger express of the type No. 104 (the Picton to Christchurch express),' he said.[6]

Gurr therefore did not lack capacity as an engine driver. While it might be said that at 29 Gurr was young for an engine driver, if at that age he did not possess all normal faculties, balanced judgement and a sense of train-running responsibility, he would never have them. Moreover, James Binstead contended it was better to send Gurr to Kaikoura than to have other drivers at Kaikoura working excessive hours.

Six perished in the wreckage of this Main Trunk express from Picton to Christchurch, when the tender and engine overturned on a curve near Seddon. Most of the casualties occurred in No. 2 and 3 carriages in the foreground.

The district mechanical engineer's opinion on the experience necessary to drive an express train was challenged by the Engine Drivers', Firemen's and Cleaners' Association, which held no driver should man a passenger train unless he had sufficient experience to qualify for the first-class driver's certificate. That would mean drivers of passenger trains would have at least 939 days' driving experience. The association had made representations for many years to the general manager of Railways on the subject and the general manager had agreed, said an association official. The only difference was that the reply had been qualified with 'where practicable'.[7]

Joseph Gurr, who was commended by the board of the inquiry for the candour of his evidence, admitted his speed into Blenheim on the journey south had been excessive, resulting in overrunning the station. But it was the first time he had driven any train in from the north.

Since his first trip as a driver in August 1946, shunting between Linwood and Christchurch, he had done four relieving trips on the Springfield–Arthur's Pass run and trips from Rakaia to Methven, to Parnassus, Rangiora and Kaiapoi. As a fireman at Ward between 1938 and 1939, he had had 30–40 trips between Ward and Blenheim and between 6 and 25 February he had driven over the curve on which the accident had happened, three times in daylight, the third occasion being with a goods train northwards on the day of the accident.

By his watch, the express train left Seddon at 11.30 a.m. In addition to five minutes lost at Blenheim he had lost time at Dashwood. The train was drifting and he was watching the track ahead, down a straight.

When he saw the 200 m (10 chain) warning board, perhaps 90 m (100 yds) off, he made a light application of the brakes, then the train was into the curve. (He had followed what would have been in his opinion the normal course for braking a goods train — a light application to bunch the train and to avoid jolts and then a further application.)

'The next thing I remember I felt a kick or surge behind me,' Gurr told the inquiry. 'I don't know what actually happened after that. I remember flying through the air. The engine went over on the fireman's side and I flew through the air to the fireman's side.'

Counsel for the Crown: 'If the train went into the curve at 55 or 60 miles an hour, you must have been very much astray in your estimate of speed.'

Gurr: 'I made a terrific error there.'[8]

Just how terrific was counted in lives lost, people hurt, wreckage and debris and a scene at the Wairau Public Hospital described as akin to the Blitz on London.

When the express left Blenheim at 10.40 a.m. it consisted of five second-class carriages, two first-class carriages, a guard's van and a Z wagon for mails and luggage, all pulled by the Ab 696 locomotive. There were only a few passengers in the first carriage but the remaining second-class cars were about half filled.

About 4 km (2½ miles) south of Seddon the express entered a cutting on a slight downgrade approaching the Blind River station. The engine had entered the 200 m (10 chain) curve, modified to 170 m (8.4 chains), and was almost out of it when the tender, then the engine overturned, rather than being derailed, an unusual juxtaposition.

The first car toppled on to the bank behind the tender, with the following three cars running past and piling up ahead of the engine. The fifth and sixth cars were totally derailed but stood upright alongside the engine and the first car. The last car survived (though derailed), while the van and Z wagon remained secure on the track. Both the second and third carriages were destroyed, the first with the roof and one side wrecked, while the third carriage, striking the second as it passed, was reduced to splintered and tangled wreckage.

'There was such a terrible shambles that there was little I could do except assist injured passengers whom I could reach,' said the guard, J. R. Parmenter, of Picton. His efforts were highly commended by passengers, and there was work enough for him.[9]

Dead and injured passengers were thrown for metres around by the impact. Others were trapped in the wreckage. Some were injured when they tried to escape clouds of steam from the wrecked engine, having to smash windows to get out. One young Rotorua woman in the second carriage was lifted bodily from her seat and hurled through what was left of a window on to the gravel at the side of the line. She was lucky.

Ambulances, farm trucks, school buses and private cars were used to transport the injured to hospital, many with morphia injections. Rescue workers were assisted by two truckloads of airmen from the Woodbourne RNZAF Station, a section of which used gas to cut off the distorted end of the third carriage, the leading end of the all-steel underframe being bent back through an angle of about 120°.

Medical staff who had been rushed to the accident scene returned to their Blenheim hospital base where 40 operations were performed on survivors over a period of 12 hours.

Predictably, the inquiry also raised the question of speedometers being fitted on all trains. But in this stand-off debate, who was right — the authorities in insisting that an acting engine driver was competent to keep a tight schedule safely on a passenger express train on a largely unfamiliar route? Or those who thought the 'safety first' principle put a premium on experience?

Chapter 3
A PERILOUS LANDSCAPE

New Zealand is undoubtedly a beautiful country. Most New Zealanders would assert that it is the most beautiful country in the world. Majestic snow-capped mountains; blue water, white sands and pohutukawa lapping the northern coasts; tall timber and low fern and lush bush; sprawling lakes, gorges and rivers, from the fast flowing to the lazy. In all, it is a country in which to rejoice.

But if New Zealand is a tourist agent's dream, it is also often a nightmare for the construction engineer, the geologist, the planner. And no less for Railways construction staff, train control officers and train crews.

Their concern is reflected in the number of rail accidents caused by slips, subsidences, washouts and floods. Nature usually paints a pretty picture in still life, but glosses over the faults until a slip rushes down a hillside to scar the grassy surface and pile up boulder-ridden debris in many a hazardous place. The very instability which plagues the New Zealand countryside can encourage a flood, cause a subsidence and, if beneath a railway line, mean another accident. And this is apart from nature's other backhanders — fog, high gusting wind, even the lahar.

Such accidents can happen, more often in the past than now when lessons have been applied, in spite of dedicated design and construction engineers who have successfully tackled the often peculiar problems of the New Zealand countryside. Worldwide recognition has been accorded their more spectacular achievements. Surveyors and engineers have shared the problem of how to limit the number of gradients on a proposed line while taking the most direct course at an economical cost. The other primary planning priority has been rail safety.

How unstable is the hillside? How exposed to gale-force wind gusts is this spiral? How prone to flooding is this river when the snow begins to melt? What is the earthquake hazard? Yet in spite of answers being sought to questions such as these, slips, subsidences and flooding have interfered with train movements, sometimes desperately, ever since the Railways opened scheduled services in New Zealand.

Today the New Zealand Railways system has a total route length of about 4600 km. Within this length there are some 2600 bridges and viaducts built to an aggregate length of 90 km, with the longest 1743 m long (Rakaia River) and the highest 97 m above the bed of the Mohaka River. Of 174 railway tunnels, the longest are Kaimai (8.9 km between Tauranga and Morrinsville), Rimutaka (8.8 km, Upper

Hutt–Featherston) and Otira (8.5 km, Otira to Arthur's Pass).

Over all these tracks, tunnels and bridges/viaducts a constant watch is maintained by gangers and platelayers who patrol on motorised trolleys or on foot, reporting any sign of landslips, subsidence or other expected trouble. Experienced and conscientious, they must have saved many an accident, many a train and perhaps many a life.

Yet with all the best intentions in the world there were mishaps, some spectacular. At Chaneys in 1905, for example, a subsidence was caused by floodwaters which 'poured with the force of a mill race through the gap'. Then there was the washout at Piriaka in the King Country in 1925 so massive that a person could 'walk right under the line which was suspended in mid-air'. Small wonder the department accepted such washouts with a certain philosophic reluctance as something properly beyond forecast or anticipation or human prevention at the time. There would be no board of inquiry in such cases because the cause was obvious and there was no human failure at any point.

Maintenance and design is now much better. Technology has improved; train crews are finely tuned. But the elements remain unpredictable. Human vigilance can function to a certain point and engineering and other precautions are marshalled to meet that point, better now than yesterday. It is yesterday's steam train accidents which show graphically the destructive force of a washout or slip.

KAIWARRA 29 March 1888

A 'black southerly buster' which brought gale-force winds to Cook Strait also brought operations on the Hutt Valley line between Ngauranga and Petone to a complete halt — for a week.

Although the track looks secure in this picture, rails and sleepers on the permanent way both before and behind this train were left suspended in the air as ballast was washed away by high seas. This train was stranded on the Wellington–Petone line for a week.

The evening train from Wellington to the Wairarapa left to timetable on 29 March 1888 and became stranded when the line was damaged both behind and in front of it. For about 1.5 km (1 mile) the permanent way almost disappeared, rails and sleepers being suspended in mid-air as ballast from under the sleepers was washed out to sea by high tides.

A workforce of 300 men restored the line, enabling traffic to be resumed on 6 April, but trains were required to travel at a very slow rate over the Wellington to Petone section. As the storm subsided, the new Wellington Opera House was destroyed by fire. Arson was suspected. As one newspaper commented, 'It has been a dreadful 24 hours in Wellington.'

A Nc engine pulling a 100 m (326 ft) long train ran into wind trouble at Makerua, 115 km (72 miles) from Wellington on the Manawatu line in 1916, when all the vehicles except the engine left the rails and capsized over a bank about 2.5 m (8 ft) high. A heavy south-east gale was blowing and it was estimated the wind pressure necessary to overturn an A car was 1.25 kg per 0.10 m^2 (3.8 lb per ft^2).

It was thought a sudden increase from 65 to 95 km (40 to 60 miles) an hour would give a momentary pressure equal to a velocity of 120 km (75 miles) an hour.

The cross marks the spot on the rear carriage where two men were almost decapitated when a Christchurch train was derailed when the embankment collapsed at Chaneys, near Kaiapoi, in 1905. Uc 369 was at one time buried by racing floodwaters.

CHANEYS 24 June 1905

Two men standing on the rear platform of the first carriage of the Christchurch to Kaiapoi midday train on 24 June 1905 were almost decapitated when the train plunged to destruction because of a flood-weakened embankment a short distance beyond Chaneys, a flag station 16 km (10 miles) north of Christchurch, near Kaiapoi.

The railway line had acted as a kind of dam as the overflow waters from the Waimakariri River spread over the level country between the river and Belfast.

Although the line had been inspected twice during the morning by a ganger on his trolley, and three passenger and two goods trains had passed over the line before 11 a.m., the midday passenger train, albeit travelling at a slow pace, proved too heavy for the weakened track.

Suddenly, engine Uc 369 sank into a depression caused by its own weight and was thrown on to its side. The brake and feeder vans next to the engine turned on their ends and the first passenger carriage ran into them.

This breached the railway embankment through which floodwaters poured with the force of a mill race, quickly submerging the engine. Driver and fireman jumped into the water and escaped without undue injury. Light and sandy soil had slowly been undermined and loosed as floodwaters gradually penetrated the railway embankment; outwardly there had been nothing to show that the track was defective. The train consisted of eight vehicles, the feeder van and a brake van being immediately behind the engine tender. Then came five passenger carriages and a van.

A schoolmaster and a farmer from Kaiapoi were standing on a carriage platform and were caught by their heads between the ends of the roof of the second and first carriages. Their heads were almost severed from the trunks. Death was instantaneous. A Kaiapoi farmer was standing on the front platform of the second carriage. When the impact happened his legs were caught in the wreckage of the carriage and both were broken.

A railway bridge inspector aboard the unfortunate train told a coroner's jury that the floodwater was 'fully' 175 mm (7 ins) below the level of the rails. He had seen no indications of any danger and did not regard the water alongside as a menace. Clay might be better than sand as material for the permanent way at the place of the accident, but sand was as good as clay for carrying weight.

The coroner's jury returned a verdict of accidental death, with a rider: 'That the attention of the Railways Department be drawn to the class of material used in the formation on the length; that it is not substantial enough to withstand the flood water which may pour at any time.'[1] The foreman added that the jury were unanimously agreed there was no blame attaching to any of the railway authorities and that the best was done under the circumstances.

ONGARUE About 1906

The rugged King Country in the heart of the North Island has always been notorious for its instability. This Edwardian mishap happened about 1906, when an old spic and span Rogers K class locomotive hauling a rake of trucks ploughed into a landslide north of Ongarue. The engine ended up in a somewhat dirty condition, considering this was an era when you could eat your breakfast off the running plate of any engine in service.

TARINGAMOTU 23 July 1915

Four nights aboard a northbound express train stranded in the King Country by unprecedented rain and floods was the unfortunate experience of passengers who reached Auckland on 25 July 1915 — three days overdue.

Six express trains were stranded between Otorohanga and Taihape and on Saturday afternoon, 24 July, Taumarunui was thronged as never before by passengers of two express trains while among the overflow passenger crowd which found refuge at Te Kuiti were soldiers, who took time out to play an unexpected rugby match with local Maoris. The Maoris won.

Relief for overburdened boarding houses and eating places at the two towns came only when four express trains resumed their interrupted journeys in a period of 24 hours, two for Auckland, two for Wellington. There were no human casualties, but two engines and a mail van fell victim to the extraordinary conditions. After a wait of 30 hours at

Taumarunui, one express train drawn by two locomotives left for Auckland. On reaching Taringamotu, 4.4 km (2¾ miles) north, the train slowed to walking pace to cross a section of sumerged track where danger was anticipated.

The two locomotives began to crawl slowly over this part of the line but, when midway across, the line sank and threw the locomotives and mail van completely over on to their sides by the river. A sleeping car, though derailed, remained in a leaning position. Landing in slush and water beside the line, the locomotives were in no way damaged. About 60 m (3 chains) of line had subsided to a depth of about 1.2 m (4 ft) below its former level. The driver and fireman of the first engine jumped clear as the engine toppled. The fireman from the second engine also jumped clear, but the driver and district engineer were rolled over in the cab. A similar experience befell two Auckland postal officials in the mail van. No one was injured.

The phenomenal rains had brought the river up against the railway line, blocking the mouth of a large culvert and forcing a diverted creek to seek its old bed which exerted great pressure on, and softened, the material below the sleepers.

The first of the northbound express trains to become stranded left Wellington at 9.10 p.m. on Wednesday and reached Auckland at 1.38 p.m. on Sunday, three days overdue. Many of the 300 passengers had spent four nights in the train.

Trouble began when the train ran into a mass of earth and boulders, one estimated at 2 tonnes, at Piriaka, 10 km (6½

Locomotives and mail van completely on their sides on the rain-sodden riverbank. The locomotive in the foreground is A 605.

miles) south of Taumarunui on Thursday morning. Subsequent delays, due to slips and a washout, meant passengers were short of food for a time. First-class passengers were fortunate in having sleeping berths, while second-class passengers had to improvise beds in their carriages. Some did not have enough money to tide them over.

When the train got moving, at 12.30 a.m. on Friday, it reached only Puketutu, to be delayed by another slip. Gas ran out and candles, in lemonade bottles, were used. Breakfast was not available until the train reached Te Kuiti at 2.30 p.m. on Friday and passengers were forced to stay there two days.

A reporter on the first work train to reach Te Kuiti from the north said there were about 500 people on the station platform when the train drew into the yard 'and they certainly were a sad looking crowd', having to sleep on the train and go into town for their meals.

Two trains which left Wellington on Thursday, at 1.15 p.m. and 9.10 p.m., were joined at Taumarunui and constituted the train which met with the accident at Taringamotu. Passengers were taken back to Taumarunui, where they remained until Sunday morning. Plans to tranship passengers between stranded trains either side of Taringamotu were abandoned when slips prevented the southbound express getting within 3 km (2 miles) of the Taringamotu blockage. So the train backed up to Okahukura, 11 km (7 miles) north of Taumarunui, where 80 passengers counted themselves fortunate in having a dining car attached. Before the trains reached Auckland, railway gangers had succeeded in clearing slips at Puketutu, Poro-o-taro, Waimiha, Piriaka, Owhango and a washout at Pohaka.

Soldiers on leave from training camps, beaten at rugby, were praised by a fellow passenger for 'their uniform good humour [which] considerably relieved the monotony of waiting for the line to be reopened'.[2]

Because the expresses were mail trains, there was some interruption to the North Island mails, minimised by Auckland mails being taken to Napier by Union Company steamer *Palcona*, from where they were taken by express to Wellington.

KAKAHI 25 May 1925

When a hillside gave way without warning of any sort on 25 May 1925, 86 tonne locomotive Ab 700 returning from Waimarino (renamed National Park) to Taumarunui at a modest speed of 9.5 km (6 miles) an hour was tossed off the rails by the slip and left upside down alongside the tracks. The accident happened between Kakahi and Piriaka.

Ab 700 had assisted the Wellington mail train from Taumarunui to Waimarino and there was no hint of trouble along the line. The slip, ill timed so far as the train was concerned, blocked the Kakahi-Taumarunui Road with debris. The driver was thrown clear but the fireman was caught in the cab and had to be released by the driver. Luckily no steam pipes broke and his injuries were slight.

Ab 700 lying nose down, wheels up, after being pushed off the line by a slip at Kakahi.

Slips and washouts throughout the King Country, as the result of very heavy rain, disrupted train services and brought long and difficult hours of extra work to weary railway gangers. 'The railways are more seriously disorganised through slips and washouts on the local section than ever before in the recent history of the main trunk service,' wrote a Taumarunui newspaper correspondent. He reported how the foundations of the line at Piriaka, near the hydro-electric works, had subsided over an area about 20 m (22 yds) wide so that one 'could walk right under the line which was suspended in mid-air at this spot'.[1]

Gangers proceeding to work between Tokomaru and Shannon the same day observed that the line across a small bridge at Kara Creek, 3 km (2 miles) on the Palmerston North side of Shannon, was a little twisted. So the express from Palmerston North to Wellington was flagged and stopped just in time. By a fortunate coincidence the limited express from Auckland was late, otherwise it would probably have run on to the bridge before the gangers went out. This train was held up until 1 p.m., when the carriages were pushed over singly, passengers walking over the bridge, which was strengthened with sleepers sent from Palmerston North.

The toppled engine K 914 of the Auckland to Wellington express derailed at Paraparaumu, with the wreck of the first carriage alongside the track.

PARAPARAUMU 30 August 1936

Given a little bit of luck, dairy farmer W. Howell might have saved the Auckland to Wellington express from being derailed after it struck a slip 400 m (¼ mile) south of Paraparaumu railway station on the morning of 30 August 1936.

While getting his cows in for morning milking, the farmer looked just before daylight to a point directly opposite his property where a slip had disfigured a sloping hillside to expose clayey soil. While he could not see if the slip had crossed the railway line, he knew it must have done so. The time was 6.23 a.m. and the express was due any minute.

'I immediately ran towards the station, nearly half a mile away,' he recalled. 'It was my intention to break the signal wire, so that the arm of the signal would go to the danger position, for I knew there was no one on duty at that hour.

'I was about 40 yards off the station when the engine whistled and a moment or so later it passed through. I waved frantically and called as loudly as I could but, with the noise of the train and the poor visibility, it was impossible for the engine crew to hear or see me. And I should think the visibility would not be more than 50 yards.'[1]

Having failed to stop the train, he sent one son to call the tablet porter and a doctor and, with another son, he reached the scene of the accident in time to see the driver and fireman crawling unscathed out of their overturned engine cab.

The slip had thrown two arms of spoil across the rails and, with limited visibility in very wet and misty weather, ploughed straight through the slip. The engine then left the rails with a lurch, heeled over to the right, broke free from the leading carriage and toppled over a 3 m (10 ft) embankment, coming to

Passengers in the first carriage collecting belongings and waiting patiently after a narrow brush with death at Paraparaumu.

rest on its side with its nose only a short distance from the road. As the engine left the rails, the corner of the tender caught the first carriage so that the roof was torn off and the walls fell on the track, leaving the interior exposed. Only the seats remained upright.

All first five carriages ran off the rails but the momentum carried them on, so that the leading carriage was abreast of the engine before it stopped. Couplings and inter-carriage platforms simply folded up and the carriages wedged themselves against each other in a mess which jammed the doorways. All the derailed carriages ended in the area of the slip, so the engine came to rest about 50 m (175 ft) from the point where the train entered the slip. Still on the lines were the sleeping cars, postal van and three luggage cars.

Of 15 passengers in the first carriage of the southbound express, drawn by a 135 tonne K locomotive (K 914), three passengers were admitted to hospital and two were treated and discharged. One passenger subsequently died as a result of injuries he suffered in the derailment. Some passengers were temporarily imprisoned in their carriages, doors and windows jammed.

C. P. S. Boyer, of Wellington, was trapped with his fellow passengers in the third carriage, until railway relief workers from Paraparaumu hacked at the doors with axes.

'With the impact and the derailment of the carriages I was hurled from my seat and I had a momentary glimpse of the carriages on either side of ours thrusting their way through the end of the one I was in. Fortunately the train pulled up . . . I looked out a window and saw earth tumbling down upon the carriage. It was a great relief when we were able to get out.

'When the passengers were all rescued they commended the prompt action of the engine crew, who handled the situation very well.'[2]

Also in the third carriage were Mr and Mrs J. Richards, of Levin, travelling to Wellington to spend a day with their son: 'We heard a crunching and splintering sound and had a sensation of going off the line. We thought the leading carriages had already done . . . The passengers in the first carriages were imprisoned for a time as the cars had been driven together. When the train came to its sudden stop it was not quite daylight and [it] was very wet and misty.'[3]

One of the few passengers in the first carriage to escape without a scratch was H. A. Milne, of Hamilton, who had joined the southbound train at Frankton. He could not understand how nobody was killed. He felt the brakes being applied and then, suddenly, the engine shuddered as it struck what he later identified as the slip. The sides of the roof of the carriage and roof piled up like matchwood. His first job was to pull a girl passenger from beneath the debris.

In joining together to remove the injured for treatment on the Paraparaumu Station platform, men were running in the rain without coats, which they had given to women and children. Berths in the sleeping cars were surrendered to the emergency. Some women survivors were in shock, but generally there was little confusion. Passengers had to wade through mud and slush when they transferred to the relief train; it was still raining heavily.

It was an accident which could have had much more devastating results, but which took its own toll. No official inquiry was held, since ordinary operating procedures had been followed by all concerned. Moreover, the accident had happened at a spot where there had been no previous trouble with shifting country.

Steel framed carriages with anti-collision ends derailed north of Raurimu in January 1945.

RAURIMU 6 January 1945

Cars with steel frames and anti-collision ends saved passengers' lives when the Wellington to Auckland express was derailed by a subsidence at 1.45 a.m. just over 5 km (3½ miles) north of Raurimu.

Six cars were derailed, two sliding 4 m (14 ft) down an embankment and coming to rest at an angle of 45°. Another carriage was suspended over a deep hole in the track, being held in position by one set of its own bogies and the unbroken couplings of the next car, which was not derailed.

The subsidence occurred on a slight upgrade, as the train with 440 passengers was running at 30 km (20 miles) an hour (the regulation speed limit for that part of the track) while passing over an embankment which carried the track across a short gully between two cuttings. The top of the embankment gave way when the culvert was unable to carry an abnormal volume of floodwater. The Ka class locomotive got across, but the leading six cars left the rails.

Two passengers were injured but, after treatment by an RNZAF doctor and nurse travelling on the train and afterwards at Taumarunui Hospital, were able to resume their journey. Most passengers were asleep when the accident happened.

'It was all so sudden I did not realise what had happened,' said Mrs J. M. Bradley, of Mount Eden, whose husband suffered a bruised toe. 'I felt a sharp jolt and remember thinking we had struck a boulder. People were thrown from one side of the carriage to the other and luggage tumbled down from the racks all over us. Some women screamed a little, which was only natural, but the menfolk were wonderful and there was no panic or commotion.'[1]

An RNZAF airman told how some passengers in his carriage cried 'Hold everything' as the car slid gently down the slope. 'We finished up at an angle of about 45 degrees and we only managed to reach the door by forming a chain and walking on the ends of the seats.'[2]

After they had been helped from the carriages, passengers sat round in groups, singing songs, for the night was warm and clear. Then all were squeezed into the remaining three first-class cars, with their luggage, for the journey back to Raurimu, where refreshments were most welcome.

MANAWATU GORGE 20 August 1946

In the then worst accident to happen to a train in the Manawatu Gorge, Ka 951 toppled down an 18 m (60 ft) bank into a flood-swollen Manawatu River at 4.17 a.m. on 20 August 1946.

The train, No. 942, was wrecked after either hitting a slip across the line or being engulfed by one in the gorge. The engine, tender and three wagons of the northbound goods train were lost and one wagon was left precariously perched

Ka 951 on its side in the Manawatu River.

across the face of the slip. The engine driver and fireman did not survive.

A large slip had fallen on the line and it appeared that the engine and leading wagons were swept over the bank by the weight of the landslide. A large boulder weighing about 4 tonnes was found near the line at the scene of the accident; the locomotive must have pushed past this obstacle for some metres before plunging into the river. Had the slip blocked the line before the arrival of the train it was more than likely that the crew would have seen it, because the accident happened on a fairly straight stretch.

Guard R. Maitland noted that the brakes had not been applied. He made his way to the front of the train but could not get round the slip which covered the line. He could see that the engine and front wagons were missing and received no

The wagon perched precariously across the face of the slip. The engine is partially submerged in the flooded Manawatu River.

response when he called out to the driver and fireman. In pitch darkness and driving rain, with the aid of only a small handlamp, the guard made a perilous ascent over the slip and continued until he came to a house near Balance Bridge, where he asked for assistance.

The train had departed from Palmerston North at 3.36 a.m. for Napier. It had nearly cleared the gorge when the accident happened about 1.5 km (1 mile) on the Woodville side of the Te Apiti siding.

It was a queer twist of fate that the engine crew who perished were from Palmerston North. Normally a driver and fireman from Waipukurau brought the goods train down from Napier to Palmerston North each Monday night and returned with it on Tuesday morning. Because of an alteration in schedule the two Waipukurau men had not come through to Palmerston North the previous night.

Retrieving Ka 951 from the riverbed proved quite a challenge. A platform was built out from the track and the engine was brought up in sections, later to run, rebuilt, on the Main Trunk line.

The body of driver Basil Craighead was found on Foxton Beach at the mouth of the Manawatu River, but that of the fireman was never recovered, presumably swept out to sea.

ANISEED 3 November 1947

The first major accident on the line north of Kaikoura since it was opened in December 1945 happened on 3 November 1947. An engine and 15 wagons, some loaded, were derailed when a goods train from Kaikoura to Blenheim crashed into a slip across the line near Aniseed, about 16 km (10 miles) north of Kaikoura.

The train was travelling at a fair pace and wagon after wagon piled up in indescribable confusion, with the engine plunging off the line, over a bank and on through several metres of the slip, coming to an abrupt stop with its nose buried in the mud. Both driver and fireman were badly shaken up and suffered shock but escaped the scalding steam when flung clear of danger as the engine lurched over.

A slip across the line at Aniseed, north of Kaikoura, caused a goods train to crash disastrously. The driver and fireman, though shocked, escaped injury.

The wagons suffered most. Carried on by their own momentum, they twisted and tore up the track as they pushed towards the trucks directly in front of them. Debris was scattered everywhere. Bogies were lying completely separated from their chassis while some wagons broke their couplings and jumped past the engine tender, turning complete somersaults before coming to a stop.

Railways staff had patrolled the line about 9.30 p.m., about five hours before the accident, although the point where the slip developed had not been regarded as particularly dangerous. The hillside had a good coating of grass and was not especially steep, but heavy rain had set in from the east two days before.

Because the slip was round a sharp corner, it is doubtful whether any train, even in daylight, would have had the slightest chance of pulling up in time to avoid the obstruction. So, as the better alternative of a sorry choice, rather a goods train at night than a passenger train in daylight.

RED JACKS 30 July 1949

Driver M. Crichton's train ploughed through surface water and mud when it was derailed near Red Jacks shortly after passing the Ngahere station on the way to Greymouth on 30 July 1949. Eight wagons and a locomotive tender were destroyed.

The derailment happened five minutes after the train left Ngahere for Greymouth with a rake of 21 wagons, most of which were loaded with coal and timber. As the train approached a swamplaned area known as Three Sisters Hill, the tender preceding the engine in the train, with no cowcatcher for protection, swerved off the line to the left and the engine followed, to pile up on top of the tender in the mud on the side of the line.

Driver Crichton, hurled into a swampy pond alongside the track, was blinded by the mud in which he was enfolded and crawled slowly through the swamp, finding the railway line with his hands. The fireman, C. Paultney, stayed in the cab and suffered slight head injuries.

With no crane on the West Coast large enough to remove the wrecked engine, a deviation was made to facilitate traffic until a crane arrived from Christchurch. Four hundred Buller excursionists returning from a Ranfurly Shield match at Dunedin were brought to Greymouth and taken to Westport by road service buses.

GOOSE BAY 7 August 1950

Following 25 mm (1 in) of rain overnight, the engine of the Christchurch to Picton express was thrown on its side and the tender and two carriages were derailed when the locomotive ploughed into a loose slip at Goose Bay, 15 km (9 miles) south of Kaikoura on 7 August 1950.

The accident might have had serious consequences — had

The damaged engine and wrecked wagons of the Blackball–Greymouth mixed goods train derailed in swampland near Red Jacks.

the tender fallen over when the engine tipped at 12.30 p.m., all four carriages might also have capsized, with potential injuries to the 90 passengers. As it was, the only injury suffered was skin abrasions to the engine driver, Harry Neill, of Rangiora.

The engine crew was able to escape from their cab without difficulty as the engine went over on to its side gradually. Most passengers did not know what had happened, feeling only a sudden jar as the train came to a halt.

RAKAUTARA 2 September 1950

Drums of petrol exploded and caught fire when 16 trucks of a 40-truck train were derailed when the engine ran into a slip at Rakautara, 8 km (5 miles) north of Kaikoura, early on the morning of 2 September 1950.

Though the engine was comparatively undamaged, all 16 trucks were more or less telescoped and the force of the smash drove one of them 6 m (20 ft) above track level. No one was injured.

The Ab locomotive involved in the Rakautara derailment and fire.

The train crew stopped a passing truck and, borrowing a portable pump, sprayed water from the engine tender on the blaze, but the fire was too intense to enable the small pump to make much impression. It was left to the Kaikoura Volunteer Fire Brigade to put out the fire, with the aid of 450 m (500 yds) of hose and water from a nearby creek.

The engine remained in an upright position, although off the rails. Some of the wagons were pushed up on to the slip itself, while other wagons were slewed on to the adjoining roadway. Contents of the wagons were strewn alongside the line, leaving heaps of flour, timber, potatoes, washing machines and Air Force equipment in unsightly confusion.

HAWERA 16 July 1956

An hour after the driver of the Wellington–Auckland express, diverted from the Main Trunk, had reported at the Hawera Railway Station what he said were 'bumps on the line' just south of the run in to the station yards, a slow-moving goods train following behind the express had its Ab engine, tender and three frozen meat wagons derailed in a subsidence of 35 m (120 ft) of the metals under their weight; underground seepage had loosened the filling. The time was 1.28 a.m. on 16 July 1956.

With the Main Trunk Line closed during the night, the north- and southbound Limited and express trains had been diverted to the Taranaki route, at Marton and Taumarunui. Although the meat special approached the level crossing at very slow speed, the engine, tender and three trucks were heavy enough to send the filling spilling out from the toe, into which the engine, tender and one truck turned over on their sides. The second truck canted over and the third truck was lifted off the twisted metals. Both driver F. Price and fireman D. Marshall went down with the overturned engine and were extricated, injured, by nearby residents who were awakened by the noise.

HIHITAHI 8 July 1961

'This might have been another Tangiwai,'[1] commented the Railways traffic officer for the middle section of the North Island Main Trunk Line, Mr F. R. Light, when the leading section of engine, tender and first passenger car left the line and plunged over a 45 m (150 ft) slope. A 40 tonne boulder was the culprit, brought down in a shellrock and mud slip near Hihitahi, 12 km (8 miles) south of Waiouru.

The 70 tonne oil-fired engine, which hit the boulder a glancing blow, went down the slope upright, driver and fireman riding down with it. Behind it, angled down the slope and still coupled to the remainder of the train, was the first passenger car. The whole length of this car was over the bank, but it, too, remained upright. Windows in the car were smashed and its occupants badly shaken, but nobody was hurt.

The overturned Ab engine pulling a meat special from Patea to Hawera derailed at a point where 'bumps on the line' had been reported.

As the engine crew made their way up the bank, the locomotive caught fire, the flames illuminating the scene, which had been pitch dark. A light rain was falling. Scrub was ignited and the Waiouru volunteer fire brigade was called to put out the fire.

The locomotive of the Wellington-bound Limited express on its side after plunging down a steep slope near Hihitahi.

The express carried a full load of 300 passengers and Mr Light, for one, considered them lucky. 'Had the boulder been another six feet out nothing could have stopped the express from smashing head-on into it,' he said. 'The whole train might have gone over the bank.'[2]

One of the few people on his feet when trouble struck this train at 3.49 a.m. on 8 July 1961 was guard R. Nairne, of Palmerston North. He was checking tickets in the second carriage, which was partly derailed. He told passengers in the first carriage to walk back through the train to safety and they calmly and quickly made an orderly retreat. 'My hands were shaking so much afterwards that I couldn't roll a smoke — a chap gave me a tailor-made,' he said.[3]

'We were all half asleep,' E. B. Stack, of Auckland, reported. 'There was a sudden jolt and a noise as if the train were sliding through gravel. I looked out the window and saw a carriage swinging sideways in front of us. We stopped with a jerk and passengers and luggage were thrown to the floor, but no one was hurt. None of us knew what had happened until I went out and then I could hardly believe my eyes.'[4]

The day after this accident another huge boulder, as big as that which blocked the line, was seen to be on the move above the same spot and was blasted away.

Locomotive Ka 945 on its side above the Waiouru-Taihape main highway.

Chapter 4
SEMAPHORE ARM TO CTC AND TWC

Signalling is the key to railway safety everywhere. In New Zealand, signals are used to control the movement of all rail traffic – from main line expresses to commuter units – so that no engine may proceed without the authority of the 'go-ahead' signal. A red light is the absolute barrier.

Motorists accustomed to traffic signals disobey them at their peril. For the enginedriver the peril is enhanced many times over, if only because of the weight of the engine and train, pounding along at a speed comparable with that on the open highway. But, whereas a car can be braked to a stop in just a few metres, a 145-tonne K steam engine took much longer to pull up. Its impact in collision was frightening, as is still the case with diesel and electric engines pulling loads of anything up to 2000 tonnes and more.

(It has been estimated that a train, when braked, could decelerate at a rate of about 3 km (2 miles) per hour per second. Thus from 65 km (40 miles) an hour it would stop in about 20 seconds. The average speed from the time the brake was applied would be 30 km (20 miles) an hour (about 9 m a second) and the train would travel about 650 m (710 yards). Therefore this should be the minimum sighting distance of any signal in such circumstances.)

Nowadays centralised traffic control (CTC) is used to operate the colour-light signals and electrically operated points on the busier main lines, and track warrant control (TWC) is being introduced to ensure safety with economy on the less busy routes, replacing the earlier train tablet system.

Both CTC and TWC are a very far cry from the primitive signal controls of the earliest operating years in New Zealand, such as the short horizontal arm or semaphore mounted on a post to simulate a barrier, or the red and green flags used in daylight, or similarly coloured lights at night, used by train guards and station staff. Signalling practice in those early days had very severe limitations. Visibility was a prime fault, for a flag held casually close to the ground, or against a varied background, could not always be readily seen. Driving rain or smoke from the locomotive were other hazards.

Nor were those early signals in any way interlocked with the points. All was to come in due course, but only after the sad experience of the accident at Rakaia on 11 March 1899 when a packed excursion train crashed into the rear of another.

Some semaphores were used at that time at the more important stations in New Zealand, but there was none at Rakaia in 1899. Five passenger trains met there that night, and the only method of signalling was by dispatching a messenger up the line with a hand lamp. According to evidence given to a Royal Commission, the red hand lamp was exhibited about 270 m from the facing points, a distance quite inadequate for protective purposes.

Although this commission was unsympathetic to the hapless driver of the second train (he was dismissed from the service when the commission's report was released), it did recommend major improvements in railways operations in New Zealand, including equipping all New Zealand Railways stock with the Westinghouse continuous brake. Its first recommendation, however, was plainly spelt out:

> First: The system of crossing passenger-trains at a station, unprovided with home and distance signals is one which should, with all possible despatch, be discontinued as dangerous. . . . every station used for crossing passenger trains, and having a resident staff, should be supplied with such signals and that where trains have to be crossed at stations without resident staff the working time-table should provide for each train coming to a stand outside these points, and specify which train was to enter the station first.[1]

Charles Henry Carter, driver of the second excursion train at Rakaia Station that 1899 night, might have been scapegoat for a railways service which had outgrown its safety rules and equipment, but he was also the medium whereby New Zealand Railways, under the direction of an energetic Minister, went to work to make operations safer. Depression conditions during the 1880s and 1890s and consequent shortage of public funds delayed the needed improvements.

Signals which interlocked mechanically with points and crossings began to appear in New Zealand in 1901, while fixed signals were provded at many more stations. So also did the vital Tyer's electric train tablet system, whereby on single-track lines only one train at a time could be allowed to occupy the line between two tablet stations. The tablet was the authority to enter that section of line, and only one tablet could be released from the tablet instruments at any one time. By 1926 a total of some 2800 km (1746 miles) of line was being operated under the tablet system.

Following the mechanical interlocking of points and signals came the electro-pneumatic system, installed at Dunedin in 1907, to ease the work of signalmen. An electric "lock and block" system of working was adopted for double lines in 1908, on the principle that only one train at a time should be permitted to occupy the block section between two signal boxes.

Prior to the introduction of "block working" following the Rakaia disaster, no train was permitted to follow another at an interval of less than 15 minutes, and elaborate procedures were laid down for the protection of any train that was delayed between stations by engine trouble or weather conditions, this protection to be arranged by the guard.

Automatic signals were first introduced in 1922, replacing the two-position semaphore type operated by wires from control levers in signal boxes at stations. The three-position colour light signals introduced in 1924 were in turn replaced in the 1930s by a new design of single-lens "searchlight" signal.

Of much more consequence in the development of safe train working on New Zealand Railways was the introduction of a system of telephonic train control whereby a train control officer in a central control office directed the movements of all trains within his defined area. Then, by 1940, came the first installations of centralised traffic control (CTC) in New Zealand, a system developed in the United States and successfully copied in New Zealand. The genesis of the programme of extension of CTC from the mid 1950s was a report, warmly quoted by the Chief Signal and Electrical Engineer, New Zealand Railways, C. R. Lovatt, in 1947, from a report of the Californian Railroad Commission:

> The tremendous increase in traffic due to the transportation of war materials and armed forces has created the necessity of expediting the movement of trains over the districts affected. This increase has necessitated a prompt decision as to double tracking v's the installation of centralised traffic control systems at strategic locations in single track main lines where studies made indicate that bottle necks were seriously hampering the orderly and expeditious movements of trains in a manner consistent with safety.
>
> C.T.C. was decided upon not only as a method of expediting the movement of trains with increased safety but also in the interests of saving for war purposes the vitally needed steel which would have been required for double tracking.[2]

And Lovatt added: 'The developments in America can be just as successful in New Zealand and the result of C.T.C. in the first country indicates that no other method of working has ever had such an outstanding and immediate result on operation.'[3]

Besides eliminating the need for staff to be located and housed at remote and isolated localities, introduction of CTC expedited the movement of trains, reduced delays, and helped to increase the carrying capacity of the lines. With CTC the train control officer has complete control through a panel of levers or switches of all main-line points and signals on long stretches of railway, sometimes more than 300 km. He can see on an illuminated track diagram which sections of line are occupied by trains, what signals are at "Stop" or "Proceed", and whether points are in normal or reverse positions. With a flick of his hand, he can direct the movement of all the trains on the line under his control.

The operator maintains his own record of the movement of trains on a large timetable graph, this activity being assisted by computer technology in the latest installations. A similar record is maintained in the train control office where track warrant control (TWC) has been introduced. The essential feature of track warrant control is that no train may enter on to a main line between stations without the authority of a "track warrant". This is issued by the train control officer and transmitted by radio or telephone to the enginedriver (now known as the locomotive engineer) in charge of the train concerned. It contains all necessary instructions as to how far the train may proceed.

Mechanical failure of signals in the past century has been a rarity in New Zealand. Accidents involving signals have usually been the result of human error: mis-reading or non-observance of the signal displayed. Neglecting to observe that the 'down home' signal was showing red brought a jury rebuke for a fireman in a 1946 collision at Papatoetoe. In another mishap (Ngahauranga 1950) the engine crew had failed to keep an adequate lookout after having passed a signal which called for a substantial reduction in speed. At Levin in 1950 a station clerk was found to have 'failed to exercise reasonable care' in that he cleared signals for a train to enter a station when the points were incorrectly set.

These are samples taken at random, with the Levin mishap freely admitted by the unfortunate shift clerk – his first signals error in 34 years with the Railways Department. The board of inquiry which sat on the accident investigation discussed how best to remove the type of what is called 'man-failure' involved in the Levin collisions. But its considerations were somewhat offset by the department's transportation superintendent, A. J. Ede, who reported that nine instances of wrong signals at crossing places over 26 years were the result of human error, and a collision had occurred in only two of these cases.

The locomotives, after their head-on confrontation at Bankside. The troop train is on the left. Wreckage of the first carriage of the Christchurch train lies in the foreground. The underframe of this carriage is under the tender of the locomotive.

BANKSIDE 29 March 1907

Lady luck certainly rode the rails the night two trains met head on about 1.5 km (1 mile) north of Rakaia in March 1907. Not a life was lost in a most spectacular collision which wrecked two trains only a short distance from a notable Rakaia disaster scene eight years before.

For five months a special train headed south from Christchurch each Thursday as far as Ashburton for the convenience of people who had visited the New Zealand International Exhibition in Hagley Park. Among the many special trains arranged for Easter traffic that weekend was a northbound train carrying volunteers for the annual Easter manoeuvres at Sheffield. The trains were scheduled to pass at Bankside, 8 km (5 miles) north of Rakaia.

The troop train, U 378, consisting of a horse box, three covered wagons fitted with wooden seats and a tarpaulin roof for the troops, a carriage for the officers and a guard's van, steamed out of Timaru Station about 8.30 on the Thursday evening before Easter. On board were detachments from the Timaru Rifles, Timaru Port Guards, Geraldine Rifles, Ashburton Rifles and Ashburton Guards, a total of about 90 men. It had also been intended to transport a number of the Studholme Mounted Rifles but, because of a misunderstanding over horse boxes, 'the corps could not entrain'.

On reaching Ashburton, Captain Hefford, in charge of the Ashburton detachment, placed his men in the front covered wagon because there was better light, but driving rain and cold temperatures brought complaints about the uncomfortable conditions. At Rakaia the troops were given permission to transfer to wagons farther down the train. All the men moved except one, who elected to stay.

Sightseers from Rakaia at the scene of the accident the next day. The vintage car in the foreground was quite modern in the year 1907.

Uc 366, which was hauling the passenger train south from Christchurch, after the collision.

The night was misty at Rakaia and lights were not visible 90 m (100 yds) away. The troop train left Rakaia after waiting about an hour, the departure time being, as far as can be recalled, 12.45 a.m. on Good Friday. As the train headed into the dark and stormy night in heavy rain, its speed was said to have been slow. Officers and men settled to sleep.

The southbound train from Christchurch, a Uc 62 tonne tender engine, with six passenger cars, was running late after stopping at several wayside stations. When the train left Christchurch, after difficulty in lighting the engine's fire, the second-class carriage behind the engine contained 24 passengers. At Dunsandel, 20 passengers alighted and the remaining four changed into a car farther back. Their desire for company saved their lives.

Instructions issued in the official train advice stated clearly that these two trains were to cross at Bankside. No railway officer was stationed at Bankside; there were no telegraph or telephone communications; no tablet system was operating. Crews appeared to have been left to act on their own judgement when trains ran late.

At the subsequent board of inquiry, much was made of relevant train advices or circulars of instructions, which were required reading for train crews. Driver McNamara, on the northbound special, was fully aware of the crossing at Bankside. His opposite number, driver Mickle, saw a reference to Rolleston-Sheffield and concluded this movement did not concern him. His guard, offering much the same excuse, argued that he had not been issued with a copy at the right time; nor had the stationmaster, Christchurch, reminded him of the crossing. Although the stationmaster was not bound to do so, such a precautionary reminder was not unusual. A pre-Easter bustle, with four or five specials lined up that night, did not allow leisure for more than immediate reminders.

The damaged front of locomotive U 378, the troop train locomotive from Timaru.

Whether the southbound exhibition special did stop at Bankside brought conflicting evidence at the inquiry. First newspaper reports said: 'The train waited some time but did not turn into a siding, as instructed, then moved on at a fairly rapid pace towards Rakaia.'[1] At the inquiry, driver and guard said they went right through. The fireman said they stopped briefly.

The troop train crossed the Rakaia bridge (on which there was an 8 km (5 miles) an hour limit anyway) at a snail's pace and was gathering speed when the other train loomed out of the darkness. Driver McNamara was able to stop his northbound train but did not have time to reverse his engine and the head-on crash which followed was heard 0.75 km (half a mile) away.

Half-asleep troops were suddenly awakened by the grinding of brakes, a horrifying lurch and the noise of breaking glass. The concussion which ricocheted through the train tossed them on to the floor. They immediately scrambled to their feet and rushed for the doors. Once outside the men were almost smothered in clouds of smoke, steam, soot and chips of wood flying through the air. The one soldier who had declined to move from the first wagon had a miraculous escape. His only injuries were a bruised shoulder and a large wooden splinter in his head. Had the first wagon been full of troops, many would have been killed, for the force of the collision drove the under part of the wagon right under the horse box, while the canopy and upper part were knocked completely off.

Both engines and carriages were badly damaged by the impact. The engine on the train from Christchurch had rebounded about 3.5 m (12 ft) and had left the rails. The tender was forced into the cab, leaving little room for the driver, who was buried by coal with his hand still holding the brake. He was extricated with great difficulty, suffering from bruises and shock. His escape was very lucky because there was scarcely room for a man to stand between the buckled framework and the boiler.

The fireman on the Christchurch train, W. McGrath, said the train was moving about 3.5 m an hour. As soon as he saw the light of the other train loom into sight through the fog, he leapt from the moving train. He was found unconscious by the side of the track among the debris.

Two ponies were the only serious casualties. One was killed outright in the horse box and a colonel's pony which was found, injured, still tethered to a section of the box among the wreckage was later shot.

As the troop train was leaving Rakaia on the unknown collision course that night, the hand of Lady Luck had made one final gesture — the colonel's groom who had travelled with the horses in the horse box, bumped into the guard while running down the station platform to rejoin the horse box. He missed it and so jumped into one of the wagons loaded with troops as the train gathered speed; the horse box was smashed to atoms.

NEW LYNN 28 May 1913

J. Benny, the driver of the northbound goods from Auckland with passenger car attached, had taken in water and had passed over the short bridge spanning the Whau Stream a few hundred metres north of the New Lynn station early on the morning of 28 May 1913. Dense fog obscured everything more than a few metres distant, but the train crew was proceeding with its routine work in the usual manner.

Driver Benny had brought the train with its long rake of trucks to a standstill close to the bridge and was waiting to proceed with shunting. An apparently distant rumble temporarily distracted him, but he did not realise it was the eight carriage train which left Henderson daily at 6.35 a.m. to carry workpeople to Auckland city.

'The first I saw of her,' said driver Benny, 'she was on the bridge. Immediately I put on the reversing gear and got my train moving backwards. We had travelled about two wagon lengths in the same direction as the approaching train when she crashed into us. Neither my mate nor I attempted to jump. We stuck to our posts and beyond the shock neither of us was hurt.'[1]

Miraculously, no one was killed, and no limbs were broken, but eight people suffered severe cuts and contusions while minor injuries were suffered by other passengers of the Henderson train.

The two engines struck with a great impact, to be brought to a dead stop, with the ends of the frames of both being crumpled and the smokeboxes smashed flat. The first carriage of the Henderson passenger train, a single-compartment, second-class car, comparatively new, stood the shock wonderfully well, but the destructive power of the collision was largely absorbed by the next two cars, of earlier construction, the third carriage in fact being an old car recently transferred to

How close the New Lynn head-on collision was to becoming a major railway disaster is suggested by this picture of the telescoped front carriages of the Henderson to Auckland passenger train on the bridge over the Whau Stream, with a 15-metre fall to the riverbed. Fortunately the wrecked carriages were not toppled from the line.

The kind of damage done to the front of a locomotive in a head-on collision.

this workmen's train because other passengers refused to travel in it. This car was driven forward by the weight behind it, to telescope the second car which, in turn, was torn from its undercarriage and forced within half the length of the third, like a huge square wedge. Although pieces of woodwork flew wildly about, the cars stayed put.

The wrecked cars had few occupants and the 25 to 30 passengers in the first carriage, a popular vehicle with regular travellers because of its cushioned wooden seats built across the car, survived the shock when the body of the carriage was torn from the underframe. Indeed, the force of the impact was such that the iron supports of some seats broke through the flooring.

The trains were scheduled to cross at New Lynn station, 16 km (10 miles). Usually the goods train, after taking water, shunted on to a side track, leaving the main line clear for the passenger train heading for Auckland city.

The bridge over the Whau Stream, north of the New Lynn station, was 15 m (50 feet) above the riverbed. The home signal stood a short distance beyond the bridge. The approach to the station from the north was by a fairly steep gradient from Scraggy Hill to a length of almost level line. The road contained several curves and in form was much like an extremely elongated S, the last curve being a short distance before the bridge.

This morning the Henderson train was a few minutes behind schedule and appears to have approached the New Lynn station faster than usual. Several passengers subsequently described how they had been thrown from their seats as the train swung round the curve near the crossing over the Titirangi Road.

The home signal had not been lowered, though the signal itself was hidden by fog. The train ran past it, because the driver could not pull up in time, although that he had tried to do so was confirmed by passengers (who felt the brakes being applied) and by two men who saw streams of sparks flying from the labouring wheels as the train rushed forward between 24 and 30 km (15 and 20 miles) an hour. The fog had made the rails slippery and the wheels did not appear to grip adequately.

There was great confusion in the first carriage when the collision took place, with almost all passengers in this car suffering cuts and contusions of some sort. Those too badly hurt to leave without surgical attention were temporarily accommodated in the ladies' waiting room. Passengers in the five other carriages escaped injury, though most were thrown from their seats and frightened.

A doctor visiting New Lynn was soon on the scene and concentrated his attention on a patient, whom he accompanied to hospital where he was admitted in a critical condition. But no further doctor was available until just after 10 a.m.

At Papatoetoe station the southbound train (at right) struck the stationary locomotive with such force that it was driven back 17 m (57 ft).

PAPATOETOE 24 August 1946

'We escaped death by seconds,' said F. Wilson, driver of a train stationary at Papatoetoe station when it was struck by a southbound train with such force as to drive it back 17 m (57 ft). 'The fireman Mr J. Bowman and I were in the cab when suddenly I saw the oncoming train,' he said. 'We jumped clear and had just about reached the fence at the side of the road when the collision occurred. We did not see the crash as we were bent on putting as much distance as possible between us and the train.'[1]

Many passengers on the southbound train had narrow escapes from death in this accident, which happened at noon on Saturday 24 August 1946. Fortunately no one died, but 11 people, including the driver and fireman of the southbound train, required hospital treatment.

The driver and fireman of the stationary locomotive would probably have lost their lives had they not leapt out just before the crash, as the back of the engine was pushed about 600 mm (2 ft) into the cab when the chassis and other steelwork was buckled by the impact.

When the two locomotives met head on, the coupling to the first carriage on the Papakura train snapped, leaving a gap of about 8 m (9 yds) to the engine. The back of the carriage was thrown on to the floor of the second one and carried away the front and one side of it for a distance of about 3 m (10 ft). The roof of the second car projected the same distance into the leading one below the ceiling, tearing through the woodwork with ease. When the bogies of the two cars met, further telescoping was prevented. The two locomotives were still locked together after the stationary train had been forced back along the line. The damage to the moving engine was surprisingly light, probably because the brakes of the stationary train were off, but the other one revealed the force of the collision.

The space in the cab had been reduced to about 300 mm

The two locomotives locked together at Papatoetoe station. The engine at right, drawing a southbound train into the station, crashed into the engine which was waiting to leave with a suburban passenger train for Auckland.

(1 ft) when the chassis and body were buckled. The front of the guard's van behind this engine was resting on the chassis of the locomotive. The carriage behind it had mounted the platform of the second car and been driven as far as the door, carrying away part of the platform.

The southbound train was headed for Papakura, while the stationary train of six carriages and van was standing on the down main line on the eastern side of the Papatoetoe railway station, leaving the track clear for the Wellington to Auckland relief express. The express was running late and passed the station at the time of the collision. The stationary suburban train was due to leave for Auckland a few minutes after the crash occurred and most of the 40 passengers had taken their seats. Several passengers in the Papakura train, who were leaving it at Papatoetoe, were standing in the carriages or walking towards the doors as the train approached the station platform. Thus the scene was set for this accident, one which could have had much worse results.

The impact of two engines colliding shook windows and doors in houses several hundred metres from the station. The sound, which was almost deafening to the few bystanders on the platform, was heard in many parts of the town and attracted a large crowd to the station within a few minutes.

Medical help was also on the scene remarkably quickly — and such help was needed. Two Papatoetoe doctors arrived within a few minutes and attended to victims on the platform or in their surgeries, until three ambulances arrived from Auckland, bringing two more hospital doctors. Five members of the Papatoetoe St John Ambulance Brigade Nursing Division, as well as local members, arrived to give first aid. After inspecting the wrecked carriages, one of the Auckland doctors, Barclay Innes (Senior Surgical Officer at Auckland Hospital) said he could not understand how anyone had come out alive from the telescoped cars, because seats and racks had been smashed to pieces.

Doctors and first aid workers found dazed and injured passengers from the wreckage of the two leading carriages of the southbound train. All were brought on to the station platform. Others who had been thrown to the floor or against seats and windows were bruised and had been cut by flying glass and splintered woodwork, but were able to go home after receiving medical attention at the railway station.

George Teriaki, who was admitted to hospital with a fracture of the spine, was sitting with his back to the engine at the very front of the leading carriage of the southbound train. He was thrown violently forward by the impact. J. J. Whale, admitted to Auckland Hospital with concussion and a fractured nose, was about to open the forward door of the leading carriage when the collision occurred. He was thrown against the door, then fell to the floor on top of a small boy who had been sitting in a seat near the door.

Some passengers had no clear recollection of what had happened. Miss A. M. Hartley, who was treated for lacerations, bruises and shock, said: 'I was sitting at the rear of the second carriage of the southbound train. I remember a terrific noise but cannot remember being thrown about. After the collision I walked to another seat and it was then I noticed I was bleeding from cuts on the face.'[2]

The guard on the Papakura train, T. Mortimer, who was slightly injured, was in his compartment at the front of the first carriage when the crash occurred. He was just opening the door on to the platform and the impact threw him from the carriage on to the station platform. He escaped with only lacerations and abrasions above one eye.

The 11 injured were transferred by ambulances to Auckland Hospital, reaching their destination soon after 1 p.m. Four were admitted and the rest treated in the casualty department and discharged.

The engineer and fireman of the southbound Papakura train were charged with endangering the safety of passengers by neglecting to observe that the down home signal was showing red, indicating danger, when they were approaching Papakura railway station. They were committed to the Supreme Court, where a jury acquitted the engineer but found the fireman guilty of causing actual bodily harm in such circumstances that if a death had followed he would have been guilty of manslaughter. The jury found that the fireman had a 'continuous and protracted view of the home signal' that was denied the engine driver, but added a strong recommendation for mercy.[3] The fireman was ordered to come up for sentence within two years if called upon.

The two Wab class locomotives locked together at Papatoetoe.

PARNELL 8 September 1947

District traffic manager Charles Lineham thought the Auckland to Waitakere train on which he was a passenger on 8 September 1947 would stop at the red over red signal just outside Auckland Station, but the train continued on. Alarmed, he got up to pull the emergency brake in his carriage — a second or two too late.

A relief express from Whangarei crossed the points from the

track on which the Waitakere train was travelling, on the Auckland railway station side of the Parnell overhead bridge. As the engine did so, the fireman of the express warned that a train was passing the other way, but the driver realised this train was moving on the same track as that occupied by the trailing end of his train. He applied his emergency brake, but his train was struck, the fourth carriage being derailed and capsized, while the fifth carriage was derailed and slewed over in front of the other engine.

The side of one carriage of the express was torn almost completely off and the 25 tonne car was flung off the track to come to rest on its side, a jumbled confusion of seats, passengers, broken timber and glass, only a few metres from a steep 6 m embankment. The impact tore loose the couplings with this carriage and that ahead of it, but the forepart of the train, with three cars, was not affected and was able to proceed to the station.

The carriage behind that was struck by the locomotive and was derailed, but the damage was confined to broken windows. The last carriage and the guard's van were not damaged. The front and side of the suburban train engine were torn out and the fireman was slightly injured, requiring casualty treatment.

Fourteen people, including the fireman of the Auckland to Waitakere train, were treated in the casualty department of Auckland Hospital and four were admitted, all with 'not serious' condition classifications. Rescue parties included uninjured passengers, the crews of six St John Ambulances which were quickly on the scene and an unnamed man at a nearby hotel, who heard the tearing crash of the collision and quickly climbed the steep embankment to smash open the door at one end of the capsized car. He found four people in this section and helped to lift them clear.

Passengers had their own moments of wonder. Constantine Marquis, of New Plymouth, whose wife was admitted to hospital with concussion, was returning to Whangarei when the train crossed the Parnell overhead bridge. He saw the other train approaching on the same line and just as he thought it was going to pass there was a terrific crash. The carriage capsized and next he was being pulled out of a window. Athol Gedy, a passenger on the Auckland to Waitakere train, was in the first carriage when he heard the brakes being applied. Then followed a series of sudden jolts and showers of splinters flying past the window. No one in his carriage was injured.

The engine driver (aged 41) and the fireman (20) were jointly charged in the Supreme Court with the equivalent of manslaughter, on which they were acquitted. On a secondary charge of culpable negligence, they were also acquitted.

LEVIN 12 April 1950

With both engines sounding their whistles at full blast seconds before the collision, a passenger train (Field's express) from Palmerston North bore straight down on the 3 o'clock

Ka 931, one of the locomotives involved in the 1950 collision at Levin.

Wellington–Auckland express stationary at Levin station at 4.50 p.m. on 12 April 1950. The two engines collided with a rending crash.

That only two people were injured in the accident was due to prompt action by the engine drivers and the crew of a goods train also stationary at the station, who noticed the points were wrong and anticipated what was about to happen. They alerted their opposites, the driver signalling the express driver to reverse, his fireman waving frantically to the Field's driver to brake. The last named had his emergency brake full on and had slowed his train from 65 to 80 km (40 to 50 miles) an hour to about 15 km (10 miles) an hour when the collision occurred. At the time the driver of the Auckland express had his train moving backwards.

Both engines were damaged, the force of the collision bouncing them back 10 m (12 yds) from each other, while the engine of the 3 o'clock was driven back into the first carriage as far as the third seat.

Luckiest man on the scene was Trooper J. B. Colville, who had been standing on the front platform of the first carriage of the Auckland express. He jumped clear. Seconds later the car platform on which he had been standing was caving in as the weight of the engine jumped back on it. 'I didn't know at first,' Trooper Colville said, 'whether to jump for it or dash in and warn the rest of the carriage. I decided there was no time and jumped.'[1] The fact that there were only 10 passengers in this carriage undoubtedly limited the extent of the injuries.

Lance Corporal A. A. Broughton saw the accident from the station platform — 'The doors of the carriage turned back, crumpled in. I saw the passengers rushing to the rear doors.

'One girl remained, though. She just sat stock-still. I think she must have been too terrified to move.'[2] Fortunately she was not hurt. Two carriages of the southbound train were slightly damaged.

Cause of the collision was the wrongful admission of the Palmerston North to Wellington train to the main line at Levin station while the express was already standing on the line, because the railway shift clerk at Levin station had 'failed to comply with the rules and regulations of the department respecting signal procedure'.[3]

The clerk freely admitted he had pulled off the main home and distant signals for the southbound train. He had noticed the permission lever in the signal cabin was reversed as he left the cabin, but as he was making for the van of the northbound express at the station with a tablet for exchange with the southbound train he did not stop to think of the lever's position.

'I can only account for my mistake as a result of an alteration in the arrival of these two trains,' he told the inquiry. 'No. 641 [southbound express] arrives first and is always berthed on the crossing loop. This means that after replacing the main line points and loop home signals and obtaining a tablet for 626 [northbound express] I lowered the main line signals for this train. I have made it a practice to check signals after both lowering and replacing the signal levers. I am unable to say definitely whether I actually checked the semaphore signals on this occasion.'[4] He had served with the department for 34 years, operating signals for most of this time without any previous error.

During the board's inquiry, the New Zealand Railway Officers' Institute submitted that had the decision been taken in 1939 to track-circuit Levin station and yard, and had such work been carried out, the 1950 collision would not have happened. The presence of trains on the sections so circuited would have been indicated on an illuminated diagram in the signal cabin and levers controlling the signals at either end governing the entrance to the lines so occupied could not have been operated.

The board of inquiry concluded:

> Full track circuiting at Levin would involve consideration of priorities, for it is clear that from the point of view of public safety many other stations have greater claims for that provision. Levin has only daylight passenger train crossings, while night crossings and difficult weather conditions such as snow or frost, etc., are features of similar stations in the middle of the North Island. . . .
>
> It may be contended that it should be mechanically possible to provide completely automatic control of trains, thus eliminating all risks of 'man–failure' in respect of fixed signals. This would, however, involve the installing of automatic train stops and the equipping of locomotives with the necessary tripping gear, which would involve extremely heavy expenditure and might expensively eliminate 'man–failure' with no certainty that 'machine-failure' is eliminated.[5]

KAUKAPAKAPA 23 December 1952

Sometimes the obvious is so wrong. When a board of inquiry into a fatal accident at Kaukapapapa station on 23 December 1952 decided that the engine crew had confused the green light on the up home main line signal with a street light which appeared as a green light some degrees to one side of the actual signal light. Whatever the reason, about 11.30 p.m. that Friday train No. 76 sailed past the signal and in a collision with train No. 77, standing at the platform, engine driver D. H. Coggins of Auckland lost his life.

Locomotive men were not satisfied with the board's finding. Not only was the dead driver respected by his peers but the surviving crew — fireman and guard — testified that the signal was clear for No. 76. Moreover, the signal levers were set so that a stop signal should have been shown. Yet the signal could not be faulted in subsequent tests.

Locomotive crews regarded this particular signal with suspicion from then on but it was not until 16 July 1953 that the engine driver and fireman of train No. 75, departing from Kaukapakapa at 2.43 a.m., found the same signal to be showing green when it should have been set on red. Signal levers were in the correct position. The same fault was observed again on 28 September 1954.

At this point the department began a keen investigation, which faulted the signal several times, so the last section of pipe housing the signal was unearthed from under the main line. Then it was confirmed that just over 1 kg of scoria ballast had intruded the pipe, some of it as much as 25 mm in diameter. The ballast had entered the open end of the pipe, eventually accumulating in a depression in the pipe and occasionally jamming the wire, prevening it from slackening back and allowing the signal to return to its normal position.

The *New Zealand Locomotive Engineers' Journal* of 1 August 1955 commented: 'While interference with signal wires is a common cause of false indications on semaphore signals, it often happens that the source of the trouble is not readily apparent, particularly if the false indication cannot be reproduced under investigation.'

This accident mystery was officially ended when the Railways Department paid the widow of Coggins the sum of $10,000 compensation, thus clearing the dead driver of any suspicion of having driven past a stop signal by confusing it with a nearby street light.

STILLWATER 11 November 1960

Three girl hitchhikers, the only passengers, were injured when the guard's van in which they were travelling was involved in a collision between two goods trains near the Stillwater tunnel on the Midland railway line on 11 November 1960.

A goods train bringing Christchurch perishables from Otira had just emerged from the Brunner tunnel about 0.5 km (¼ mile) west of Stillwater from which a goods train proceeding from Greymouth to Blackball had just departed.

Seven wagons on the Blackball train were derailed, as well as a van and two box wagons on the train from Christchurch. The westbound locomotive climbed up on to the Blackball locomotive and the wagons telescoped behind both twisted units.

The girl passengers — aged 19, 18 and 18 — were seated on the right-hand side of the van and almost in front of them the twisted steel of the tender rammed back through the van, converting the left-hand side to matchwood. The girls were huddled next to the jagged steel ends. No one on the other side could have survived. It was here that the guard had been seated, but he had risen to prepare a bundle of newspapers for delivery at Brunner, only to see the area he had left obliterated by tonnes of steel.

A departmental inquiry found the Blackball-bound train had wrongly passed the automatic departure signal at Brunner.

The head-on collision between two goods trains near the Stillwater tunnel.

Chapter 5
MANNING THE SYSTEM

Fewer people are now employed to make the railways work. Where historically we talked of 'train crews', since 1988 a train will often be found to be worked by just one man, the engine-driver or 'locomotive engineer'. With electrification and the switch on other lines to diesel power, the fireman became for a time the 'locomotive assistant' until the advent of radio communication made this position redundant. The guard went with the removal of guard's vans, although his shadow lives on as 'train manager' on passenger trains. Many other time-honoured designations have also been changed, all part of the reshaping of railway services in economy moves which have cut the workforce on the NZR from 22,000 in 1982 to fewer than 9000.

Our concern in this book however is with the men and women who used to make the railways work, in particular the men on the footplate of the steam trains of the past.

The guard was the senior officer of the train, responsible for overall authority, for departure signals and braking in an emergency, the confidant of stationmasters en route, the officer who made the reports. It was the engine crew, however, who invariably attracted the glamour spotlight, won the respect of males young and old. For who couldn't admire the men who drove these monsters of 'majestic power, imperious progress and sounding fury'?

The seemingly casual, chin in cupped elbow, peaked cap above eyebrows appearance of an engine driver waiting his passengers to board is the typical memory of the steam train driver. Mostly he was a friendly soul, ready to share his wisdom with the casual inquirer, invariably from the authority of his cab, unless he paused somewhere en route while oiling con rods or other mysterious parts and was as interested in his engine as his curious passengers.

The fireman was only a little below the status of the driver in travellers' respect. He was another expert in the cab whose job was to build up the steam power enough to make the engine do its job. His could be hard work, especially with a heavy train on a hard grade. (One of the authors, with an Air Force companion, at the beginning of 1940, fired an overnight passenger express between Oamaru and Timaru, to the amusement of the train crew — and finished dirty, exhausted and with an immense respect for the sheer muscle power of the one fireman who could move more coal than we could together.) For many firemen, their job was a halfway point in their railway careers, a graduation from the bottom rung of engine cleaner to that of engine driver. It was very much a matter of learning from the bottom up!

In the years when steam was king the Railways youth entrant sank or swam according to his own capacity and initiative, learning by precept rather than by correspondence courses, introductory sessions and seminars. He usually began as a cleaner, looking after the boilers in the sheds, in the bigger depots part of three daily shifts, rotating round the clock. In the Auckland depot, for instance, 40 years ago or so, there could be 12 rows, with four cleaners responsible for three rows each, each with his own engines. If a man was on a day off, that engine stayed in the shed; nobody else touched it.

Washout men were at a lower level still, mostly casual staff, who climbed into the fireboxes for 10–14-day inspections and, if there was a defect, renewed the bricks and so on.

From cleaner status, the ambitious employee proceeded by examination (mainly on signals) to a fireman's shunt ticket, which allowed him to fire on yard shunts only, thus relieving a qualified man to do main line work. To qualify for this, the fireman had to sit the full fireman's examination.

If he qualified, it was usually about another seven years before he would be allowed to sit the second-grade engine driver's certificate, and then begin over again in yard shunts, suburban shunts and eventually goods trains. Only when he had passed his first-grade ticket was he allowed to drive passenger trains.

Since the years of steam the engine crew has changed to consist of a driver and a locomotive assistant. Opinion seems divided on the degree of responsibility between steam and diesel unit operation. Diesel locomotives are more complex because of circuits, circuit breakers and other electrical equipment, but their safety devices are more generous, vigilance devices crowding on the crew. Time signals, which apply emergency brakes automatically if not acknowledged are an immediate safety precaution, while the deadman's pedal will stop a train if foot pressure is removed.

Performance is very different now from what it was before 1950, when the Minister of Railways, the Hon. W. S. Goosman, was able to report satisfactory progress on the fitting of speedometers to locomotives, railcars and multiple unit coaches. At that stage 130 locomotives and 53 other units had been so fitted, while 151 instruments of a satisfactory type were available for fitting to other express locomotives. Until then the driver had had to estimate his speed on the basis of experience — and good luck to him! Successive boards of inquiry became increasingly impatient with the lack of a reliable instrument to measure speed as a safety aid.

Engine drivers were supplied with *Rules and Regulations,* a book, as well as the official working timetable for their area, which indicated the points between which speed limits operated. They ignored them at their peril. For instance, rule 154 of *Rules and Regulations 1943* said:

> Engine drivers must not exceed the maximum rates of speed shown in the speed schedules in working time-tables and must

> regulate the speed of their trains by the time-table, from which they should vary as little as possible. Lost time may be made up only provided the maximum speed is not exceeded.

Yet pride spurred the efforts to keep the timetable, for a variety of reasons — passengers' timetables, crossing times, the ability to keep schedules, the very essence of railways efficiency.

Drivers had, of necessity, to be selective in deciding on stretches where there was the opportunity to make up time. Drivers familiar with the route knew and nursed these opportunities, and they kept their reputations for efficiency. But if the weather was bad, too many curves bent the track, a crossing was delayed or the load too heavy, too bad — the train would be late.

Driver and fireman shared the footplate. Naturally they needed confidence in each other to perform adequately, while the very fact of sharing shifts through time implied a degree of mateship. How often an accident meant severe burns from broken engine steam pipes, to both men. Typical would be a Central Otago accident in which Ab 779 was derailed running light from Milton to Lawrence in 1961. When the engine overturned the fireman 'was buried in ballast . . . and was assisted by the driver to uncover himself. Several steam pipes were broken and both men suffered shock, concussion and minor burns'.[1] Sometimes the disfigurement was horrendous but time and again a footplate crewman went to the rescue of his mate in spite of the spitting steam.

It would be invidious to compare the men of steam with those of diesel or electric units — needs differ. But it could perhaps be argued that the farther back in time one goes into operations of the New Zealand Railways, the more demanding the work was of the engine driver and his fireman companion. Both of course shared a high degree of responsibility, a pounding trainload of human beings whose trust in the crew up front meant they were transported across viaduct, plain, curve and through tunnels at speeds which gave an awesome look to the thundering, gleaming monsters which were the engines, with their spilling smoke clouds, boasting plumes of victory. Make one mistake — one of the mistakes listed elsewhere in these pages — and limbs and freight were sprawled all over the countryside, rails twisted and bent, wagons and trucks splintered, glass shattered, passengers dead and dying.

The wonder is that, through time, the Railways have proved so safe and, in recent years, increasingly so. For as good as the system undoubtedly is, it can be only as good as the men who work it, not least those who laboured on the steam footplates or man the cabs of today's more placid engines. When, in a time of rapid expansion a decade ago, the Western Australian ore mines wanted more expertise in the handling of their train, where did they go to seek staff? New Zealand, of course.

New Zealand railwaymen can hold their heads high. Were it not so, now and in the past, how much more horrendous would be this account of misadventure on the track? Dwelling on the exceptions perhaps highlights the commonplace — of responsible men, responsible administration, well-tended rolling stock and track, and a care for passengers.

MAMAKU INCLINE 3 August 1907

Three times the engine driver sounded his locomotive whistle, each time in groups of three, and the sound carried loud and sharp on the clear frosty night to a guard who responded immediately to this injunction to apply brakes. He did so, but to no avail. Within half an hour he was dead.

Guard Jack Lowe did not know the two engines pulling his 31 rolling stock train had been detached on the Mamaku incline, about halfway between Putaruru and Mamaku. Certainly the engine crews had applied the Westinghouse brake (an 'up-to-date quick action automatic continuous airbrake') and had reinforced this by screwing down the handbrake on the leading van and pinning down the brakes on the three wagons, precautionary action which, they thought, would be more than sufficient to hold the 230 tonne train. They then went about the task of trying to find what had gone wrong with the second locomotive.

Twice one driver looked back to make sure the train was safely anchored. His second glance froze — the train was moving down the incline, on a grade of 1 in 36. He shouted a warning to his fellow driver and both jumped into their cabs to begin a futile chase. The runaway outpaced them and crashed to destruction after failing to take the second curve of a hazardous S curve at something approaching 125 km (80 miles) an hour.

Thus ended the journey on 3 August 1907 of what had been, in effect, a double train, for two trains and engines bound for Rotorua had been shunted into one train at Putaruru. When marshalling was completed under the direction of Guard Lowe, the train consisted of two locomotives (J 84 and T 102), a van, 28 trucks/wagons, a passenger carriage and a guard's van. The train was fully equipped with Westinghouse brakes and each vehicle, including the engines, was also fitted with the usual handbrakes.

As was customary at the start of a journey, the brakes were tested at Putaruru and found satisfactory. Guard Lowe signalled this from his van, which meant that the Westinghouse brake, operated from the lead engine, was operating satisfactorily throughout the train.

At 7 p.m. the train left Putaruru for Ngatira, where it stopped for a few minutes to fill the water tanks on the engines before climbing the incline towards Mamaku. This was hard work. Not only was there a lot of uphill pulling, with a rise of about 350 m (1200 ft) between Putaruru and Mamaku, but the load was heavy — though not excessive for the two locomotives. Moreover, frost had made the rails slippery, so progress on the incline was slow and careful, at a speed of

The widely strewn wreckage of the mixed goods train which ran away 10 km down the steep Mamaku incline in August 1907. On the right is the S curve, which proved too sharp for the runaway train.

The leading engine J 84, which was driven by John Taylor on the night of the runaway.

The second locomotive T 102, which gave trouble on the incline. This brought about the uncoupling of the train, leading to the sensational runaway.

Splintered wreckage of the guard's van showing the handbrake pillar at which Guard Lowe stood until his death.

something like 6–8 km (4–5 miles), with both engines puffing heavily.

Three km (2 miles) from where the train would have been over the worst of the hill, the driver of the second engine, Thomas Cooper, noticed his engine had gone off its beat (the regular 'puff, puff, puff'). An irregular beat might mean a coming breakdown of the motion machinery on one side.

The proper reaction in such circumstances was to signal the leading engine driver, John Taylor, to stop, so the trouble could be investigated. This Cooper did, and Taylor immediately applied brakes, bringing the train to a halt. Both drivers inspected locomotive T 102 for the cause of the trouble and Cooper crawled under the engine to examine the link motion for possible damage. He was under the locomotive for about five minutes, but could find nothing wrong.

So they decided to uncouple the locomotives from the train and move them slowly ahead for a closer examination. Brakes were reapplied to the train, including handbrakes on the leading wagons, the locomotives were uncoupled and the firemen drew the engines slowly forward up the line while the drivers watched for the defect.

About 65 m (70 yds) from the rest of the train, Driver Cooper looked back for reassurance that it was standing, properly held. Instead he saw it running backwards at a good speed, being between 150 and 180 m (150 and 200 yds) away. He shouted to driver Taylor that the train was moving and both men jumped on to the engines and gave chase, after Cooper had whistled to alert the guard. Then he climbed over the back of the coal tender ready to drop the coupling hook and couple the Westinghouse brake hose.

The runaway section had too great a start, however, even after the two engines had reached a speed of between 65 and 80 km (40 and 50 miles) an hour. After about 3 km (2 miles), driver Taylor eased up at Ngatira, but drove on at fast safety speed.

In the guard's van at the rear of the train were the guard, Jack Lowe, acting guard, James Dwyer, porter, Charles Tyler and a platelayer, James Kingdon. In the first-class passenger carriages were Willis Arthur McCommons, of Christchurch, general manager of the International Harvester Co. of New Zealand, Abraham Purser, of Palmerston North, a traveller for the Harvester company, Dr Engleberger, of Matamata, and Peter Dromgool, a surfaceman on the railways, who lived at Matamata.

Guard Lowe and acting guard Dwyer, and the passengers, did not know of the uncoupling. Even when the unengined train began moving, quite smoothly about 8 km (5 miles) an hour, they thought the backward movement was to win room from which to tackle the steep grade ahead. Then came the telltale triple-linked whistle alarms and the truth was out. 'We have broken loose,' said Willis McCommons. And later, 'It is all over.'[1]

In the guard's van the Westinghouse indicator went down quickly, soon reaching zero, and a minute later the train began moving backwards. Then, when the triple whistle signals were heard, an unsuccessful attempt was made to apply the Westinghouse brake. Immediately the two guards applied handbrakes, in the van and in the neighbouring carriage, but the heavy load and the steep incline were too much and the train gathered speed — backwards.

They passed Ngatira at 110 km (70 miles) an hour, still gathering speed. The passengers remained cool, two winding the carriage windows down and steadily gripping their seats as handholds, while another sought refuge by lying on the floor. In the van, James Kingdon ventured the opinion they were rushing to their destruction, but Guard Lowe was optimistic: 'If we get round the next curve we are right.'[2]

His hope was in vain. At the next curve, the bottom of the S, the van (which was leading) derailed and struck the bank with a sickening rush, to finish standing right up on end. The rest of the vehicles were thrown over the embankment and into the gully. The four men in the guard's van suffered most and Guard Lowe died 15 minutes after being extricated from the wreckage.

The carriage, when it smashed into the guard's van, was splintered to pieces, but surfaceman Peter Dromgool rolled down the embankment with hardly a scratch. Dr Engleberger, though covered in splinters, also escaped and quickly helped with the freeing of other passengers. He also attended the injured. Both the International Harvester representatives, Willis McCommons and Abraham Purser, were badly bruised as the train took its last plunge. They were thrown heavily among the wreckage and Kingdon was seriously injured. Fortunately the carriage roof remained intact, thus helping to save the lives of the passengers.

Fire broke out among the wreckage, which contained general merchandise, coal, firewood, lime and hay. Cattle trucks also suffered damage, with 45 beasts killed instantly or

Only the roof and the floor of the one passenger carriage remained intact after the smash. Wagons piled round it in wild confusion. Miraculously, nobody in the carriage was killed.

subsequently destroyed. Thirty-seven were saved.

The runaway train had covered a distance of 10 km (6¼ miles) before it left the line, of which about 16 m (6 chains) had been torn up.

An inquest into the disaster was opened in Rotorua three days later, at which both drivers were prime witnesses. John Taylor, driver of the first locomotive, described the precautions taken by driver Cooper and himself before the locomotives were taken off the train. He had recharged the Westinghouse airbrake and had uncoupled it himself and had shut both taps, one on the engine, one on the van, then for good measure had pinned down three handbrakes on the leading wagons.

Driver Cooper confirmed that no signal had been given to the guard up to the time the engines had been cut out from the train, because it was not usual to notify any stoppage until they had found that the engine had broken down and that he would be required to protect the train. What puzzled him was why the train should have run away with the Westinghouse airbrake applied, because he considered it sufficient to hold the train for an indefinite period. Driver Cooper also reported that the valve choke on his engine had accidentally cracked on the night of the accident, to make his engine go off beat. (Only five days afterwards, on its next heavy loading, the engine had broken down altogether in the Franklin yard and could not be removed, one way or the other.)

James Dwyer, the acting guard, whose evidence was taken at the hospital, had heard no release of brakes in the guard's van but felt the train moving backwards. He made a grab at the brake, but guard Lowe said it was 'all right' and he did not apply the brake. When they heard the whistle, which meant

The 28 wagons which formed the largest part of the train piled up on top of one another in bewildering confusion after leaving the rails. Some contained cattle and 45 head were killed or had to be destroyed. Hay and coal in other wagons caught fire.

'Brakes', he put on the handbrake, while Lowe rushed through and put on the carriage brake. When the train started rolling back, Dwyer was under the impression the engines were still coupled and they were only going back to get a better start up the hill. He did not know the engines were uncoupled until pulled out of the wreckage.

Willis McCommons told how he had been thrown endwise, striking a partition and being driven right through the floor of the car. He had travelled considerably and had felt the Westinghouse brake hundreds of times. Brakes made considerable concussion when applied and he had no doubt whatever that the Westinghouse was not applied.

When the evidence was completed, the jury retired, but for a brief two minutes, going out at 6.29 p.m. and returning at 6.31 p.m. The evidence, in the opinion of the jurors, was too conflicting to justify a decision as to why the train broke away.

An inquiry ordered by the Minister of Railways into the cause of the accident was held in Auckland before District Judge Charles C. Kettle. In evidence before this inquiry, Alfred L. Beattie, Chief Mechanical Engineer for the New Zealand Government Railways, said the Westinghouse brake was amply sufficient to hold the whole train on the Mamaku grade (for a certain period), provided the brake was in good order and condition. Since this braking system had been introduced into New Zealand in 1901, some 23 million train miles had been run with only one failure reported, and that due to negligence. He was satisfied this was the best possible brake the department could have, its action being automatic. In his opinion the drivers had certainly made an error in judgement in uncoupling before communicating with the guard.

Guard Jack Lowe, who was killed when the runaway train crashed at the S curve. His previous efforts to stop the train, by applying brakes, were ineffective.

Edward Harris, stationmaster at Putaruru, recalled watching Guard Lowe test the brakes after the train had been marshalled at Putaruru. Railway porter Tyler, who had travelled on the ill-fated train, confirmed the brake testing at Putaruru — 'I know for certain the brakes went on the carriage and the rear guard's van for, after I heard the clap of air concussion, I turned my lamp upon the wheels and saw the brakes act.'[3]

Fresh evidence came from a bushman, Michael Boyle, who said that about a year before he had seen a large number of Maoris jumping from the station platform at Ngatira across the couplings of the train. One of the Maori boys, in jumping across, had turned one of the taps into a horizontal position. He had drawn Guard Lowe's attention to the mishap.

This theory was also referred to by R. E. Robertson, inspector for the Westinghouse Brake Co., who said it was quite possible if Maori children were running about the trucks for them to close the cocks. 'I do not say for one moment that the children closed the cocks; but assuming they did so, then it would explain the accident. That is the only theory I have formed,' he added.[4]

In his report to the Minister, Judge Kettle wrote: 'If the guard had been consulted by the engine drivers, and if a careful brake test had been made by them before the engines were detached, all such omissions or defects, if they existed, would no doubt have been immediately detected and remedied.'[5]

What happened to the Westinghouse brake on the incline that night? Experts called to give evidence unanimously praised the Westinghouse braking system as the best in the railway world. All agreed that the brake would hold a train with ease on the grade in question from half to three-quarters of an hour. Had a brake valve tap been accidentally turned off in the front part of the train? Or had children jumping across the couplings from the station platform at Ngatira knocked one of the taps, so shutting off the air pressure? Whatever the cause, fate was kind; only one man died.

TE RAPA 2 November 1934

A terrific impact resulted when a *New Zealand Herald* train consisting of a heavy Ab engine, 706, four passenger coaches and a guard's van, ran through the Te Rapa station at 6.30 a.m. on 2 November 1934 to crash into the rear of a long goods train just moving out of the station. The engine ran through the guard's van at the back of the goods train and smashed a number of empty box wagons included in the train. The carriage immediately behind the engine of the *Herald* train was thrown completely over the locomotive and the engine was thrown on to its side. A heavy fog hung over the accident scene.

Occupants of the two trains had miraculous escapes from death. Of the seven passengers on the *Herald* train, two who had been seated in the front carriage from Auckland to Huntly decided to look for more comfortable seats after leaving Huntly and moved farther back. All the passengers were in the last

Engine driver and fireman crawled from this damaged engine unharmed after Ab 706 crashed into an almost stationary goods train at Te Rapa station, 9.5 km (6 miles) north of Frankton, while carrying passengers and copies of the *New Zealand Herald* to southern parts of the province on 2 November 1934.

two carriages when the collision happened and, beyond being thrown from their seats and feeling slightly dazed, escaped injury.

Eye witnesses were amazed to see the driver and fireman of the capsized engine, E. Marks and A. Reid, emerge from the cab unhurt. Because the capsized engine was not flat on the ground, there was just enough room for them to make their escape. The strength of the cab saved their lives. Later they drove a train back to Auckland.

Guard Percy Johnson, of Frankton, was standing alongside his van of the goods train after having signalled the driver of the train to proceed. The train had begun to move and he was about to jump into the van when he saw the other train approaching. He ran clear just in time.

The scene at the station after the accident showed the guard's van of the goods train and the first carriage of the other train completely enveloping the capsized engine, which had been very extensively damaged. The superstructure of the van and carriage was completely torn away from the chassis and the woodwork had been smashed to pieces. The next two carriages were badly damaged and derailed, although the last carriage and van of the second train escaped damage. One box wagon of the goods train was tossed completely off the line and smashed, another was piled on top of it and a third had torn up the track and been smashed. Altogether nine box wagons, all unladen, were smashed beyond repair. The track was damaged for 55 m (66 yds).

The only casualty was a pedigree Tamworth sow, owned by Dr G. Walker, of Whangarei. The animal was killed.

WHANGAMOMONA 21 December 1934

'There's going to be a crash in the Whangamomona tunnel in 10 minutes,' the officer on train control in Wanganui told his District Traffic Manager early on the morning of 21 December 1934. And about 7 a.m. a head-on collision duly followed at the northern portal of the tunnel. No one was hurt, but several goods wagons were severely damaged with many tonnes of coal and merchandise lost. Had the trains met head on in the long tunnel it is doubtful if the engine crews would have survived. They were lucky that morning.

After the Marton to Taumarunui route was adopted for the Main Trunk railway, Taranaki interests agitated for a more direct link to the Auckland province and on 28 March 1901 the first sod of the Stratford Main Trunk was turned. By 1914 the railway had reached Whangamomona, a small village in the midst of very rough country covered by virgin bush and home to wild pigs. It was said that people, especially train crews, shuddered when the name Whangamomona was mentioned.

Coal seams were discovered in the Tangarakau area, 21 km (13 miles) farther east in 1926 and a beginning was made on developing these deposits on a commercial basis. Tangarakau became the headquarters for coal operations and railway track gangs. (It might be noted that the Stratford Main Trunk was known as the 'Stratford Underground', because there were 24 tunnels from Kiore, 30.5 km (19 miles) east of Stratford, to Okahukura, a distance of 112 km (70 miles). This line was completed in 1935, years overdue.)

This shorter route for goods from Auckland to New Plymouth to towns as far south as Patea, plus the coal traffic from Tangarakau, called for many special trains to move the tonnage over the very hilly and steeply graded country between Okahukura and Stratford and vice versa. This 145 km (89 miles) of railway with 19 stations had no signalling system and was worked by what was called 'open section working'.

The head-on collision between the two trains just outside the Pohokura end of the Whangamomona tunnel was the result of several factors.

A regular timetabled goods train with a passenger car attached crossed the Auckland to New Plymouth express at Stratford and departed for Taumarunui (its timetable number being 521) at 5.26 a.m. on Friday 21 December 1934. This was a long train made up of empty goods wagons, a few loaded wagons, a passenger carriage and a guard's van. The locomotive was a heavy type Mountain X class engine. The guard was Tom Henderson, of Stratford.

No. 521 had the line to itself until it reached Pohokura, where it was timed to cross a special goods train. This train, working under the designation of No. 556 RR ('run when required') only ran when tonnage was offering, usually coal from Tangarakau.

All went well for No. 556 on this trip and guard Laurie Bate called train control from Whangamomona and was advised

X 597 (left) in an unexpected meeting with Bb 635 at the northern portal to the Whangamomona tunnel. A minute or two earlier and a costly pile up would have happened within the tunnel.

that the crossing with No. 521 would take place at Pohokura, as scheduled. In turn, train No. 521 duly arrived at Pohokura and guard Henderson reported to the train control operator, Tom Cullen, in Wanganui, and inquired how No. 556 was running.

After being told that No. 556 was on time and that the scheduled crossing would take place, and a moment or two or three passing the time of day, guard Henderson stepped outside the shelter shed — to see his train disappearing, the very same train which was to have awaited the crossing with No. 556 at that spot, Pohokura.

Train control operator Cullen absorbed the bad news quickly, then telephoned his manager at home, forecasting the head-on collision. Fortunately, engine driver Charlie Peddie had kept the old BB engine on No. 556 up to a fair speed and had nosed his way outside the tunnel.

At the official inquiry, guard Henderson admitted he had heard a slight rattling of the goods wagons while he was speaking to train control, but had thought it was the engine driver positioning his big X class engine correctly under the water tank before climbing towards the tunnel. The engine crew were adamant they had seen an arm held horizontal from a position near the guard's van. This was not sufficient authority for No. 521 to proceed, because they would have had to be shown a copy of the crossing order issued by train control if the crossing had been changed.

Whangamomona was an unkind depot for locomotive men. Engine driver Harry Kelly was killed in the Tahora yard and is buried at Whangamomona. Engine driver Jim Foreman was killed going up the section of line towards the Whangamomona tunnel and later the then fireman at this depot, engine driver Charlie Parker, was killed on the Auckland express at Tangiwai on 24 December 1953.

K 900 lying on its side after capsizing south of Mercer. The carriages ran past the engine, losing side panels from a projecting corner of the tender. This locomotive, the largest built for the North Island Main Trunk, after being on public display at Pacific Steel, Otahuhu, was presented to MOTAT by New Zealand Railways in 1968 and is now on display at Western Springs.

MERCER 28 October 1940

No one will ever know why the Wellington to Auckland express was being driven at such speed over a 160 m (8.2 chain) radius curve just south of Mercer in the early morning of Labour Day, 28 October 1940. A board of inquiry estimated the speed of the train at this dangerous point at 88 km (55 miles) an hour, yet the driver was experienced and competent. He knew the track and the need for caution at this point which was, of course, highlighted by the radius warning boards.

So why did driver J. C. C. McCubbin proceed at such speed? No one will know, because both driver and fireman were killed outright in the crash, the only fatalities. Twenty-one passengers were injured.

The schedule for the Limited express provided for a non-stop run between Frankton Junction and Auckland, including a time of 63 minutes for covering a distance of slightly under 65 km (41½ miles) between Frankton Junction and Mercer. Some observers thought this a tight schedule, which would require the maintenance of speeds approximating to the maximum speeds permitted by the official working timetable.

An examination of the 1940 schedule shows that the scheduled running time could be reduced to 55.8 minutes, plus another 0.9 minutes allowed for a speed restriction which no longer applied because of a replacement bridge. This slack could of course be used by a driver to make up lost time. But temporary special speed restrictions increased the minimum permissible running time to 59.7 minutes and reduced the

The derailed engine lies on its side, with, beside it, one of the carriages propelled forward by the force of the crash.

slack to 3.3 minutes. In other words, only 3.3 minutes of lost time could have been made up that morning by the express between Frankton Junction and Mercer without exceeding permissible maximum speeds.

On the basis of information passed to the train control office in Auckland Railway Station from six officered stations between Frankton Junction and the point of derailment, express train No. 688 was 12 minutes late leaving Frankton Junction. By the time it reached the point of derailment, 11½ minutes had been made up.

If it had been driven according to the instructions in the working timetable and in the train advices regarding special temporary speed restrictions, it could have made up only 3.3 minutes of the lost time. Records showed the train had made up no time until Ngaruawahia, so it was obvious that 11½ minutes had been made up between this station and the point of derailment, a distance of 50 km (30½ miles).

There was no need for this desperate effort to make up time before reaching Mercer for, from that station to Auckland, a matter of 70 km (43 miles), ample opportunity was available to make up time in the usual running conditions. So, why this desperate effort to recapture lost time?

Three possible explanations were explored. First, train No. 688 was 12 minutes behind schedule when it left Frankton Junction. In fact, the record entered by driver McCubbin in his running book indicated he thought the train was 14 minutes late, having inserted the time of leaving Frankton Junction two minutes later than in fact the train did. Second, 28 October

1940 was Labour Day and a holiday. Train 688 had to cross a race train and other holiday traffic between Mercer and Auckland; was the driver anxious to make up lost time to avoid delaying other traffic? Third, had the lost time not been made up on a section on which the line was fairly clear of other traffic, might the express have lost more time before it reached Auckland, thus disorganising even more the holiday arrangements of passengers?

Yet could such considerations persuade a 'steady, competent and experienced driver, with a first-class record',[1] deliberately to drive his train over a 160 m radius curve at a speed he must have known was almost certain to cause a disaster? He entered the curve, which had a fixed permanent speed restriction of 50 km (30 miles) an hour, at more than 80 km (50 miles) an hour.

Driver J. C. McCubbin, in charge of the Limited express from Wellington to Auckland on Labour Day 1940. Neither the driver nor the fireman survived, so the cause of the accident, apart from excessive speed, remains obscure.

Immediately before this restricted section was a 300 m (16 chains) curve where the maximum permissible speed was 70 km (45 miles) an hour. If express No. 688 was being driven at 70 km an hour, there should have been no difficulty in reducing speed to enter the 80 km (50 miles) an hour restricted curve, even though this would have involved a brake application somewhat heavier than the ordinary service application for which a distance of 170 m (560 feet) was required to reduce speed by 24 km (15 miles) an hour. Only 140 m (480 ft) were available to train 688; even so, if no more than an ordinary service application had been made it would only have meant the train would have entered the 160 m radius curve at a speed slightly above the authorised speed but well within the margin of safety.

There was another consideration. Driver McCubbin had been off duty for two months in 1939 with heart troubles. He was certified by a Hamilton doctor in January 1940 as having completely recovered and being fit for duty. The board of inquiry heard evidence that he appeared to be in his normal health and spirits immediately before train No. 688 left Frankton Junction on Labour Day 1940.

The board concluded:

> If the evidence of his driving at speeds markedly in excess of those permitted had related only to the last few minutes before the engine entered the 8.2 chains radius curve, it might have been possible to assume that driver McCubbin had suffered a sudden severe heart attack which had incapacitated him. As, however, the evidence is indicative of the maintenance of consistently high and excessive speeds from Ngaruawahia onwards, we are not justified in assuming that the failure of driver McCubbin to reduce speed to 30 miles an hour before entering the 8.2 chain radius curve was due to a sudden seizure.[2]

Whatever the explanation of this extraordinary speed at a sensitive section, none of the 161 passengers was killed, although the accident was spectacular enough.

The couplings and brake hose between the tender and the leading car parted, with the locomotive travelling over the sleepers and ballast after leaving the rails for some 12 m (40 ft), then along the bank for a further 38 m (125 ft), part of the time in a giant slide on the mud surface.

The impetus of the train sent the carriages forward, the leading carriage to a point 1645 m (514 ft) beyond the point of derailment. As they passed the derailed locomotive the carriages were stripped of huge sheet steel on their left sides by the rear edge of the tender, while the engine wheels ripped the interior laminated woodwork and smashed seats. The leading bogie of the leading car, after it was derailed, ploughed obliquely along the track and recrossed the rails, its wheels digging up the ballast for a considerable distance.

Discipline among passengers was excellent, with a complete absence of panic.

The chairman of the board of inquiry and one member of the three-man tribunal had also sat on the inquiry into the derailment at Ratana on 26 March 1938. The Ratana findings included a recommendation that all engines used for hauling express, mail and passenger trains be equipped with recording speedometers. Not surprisingly, perhaps, this opinion was endorsed by the tribunal which sat on the accident of Labour Day 1940. While a number of locomotives had been so equipped, the outbreak of war had made it impossible to import the preferred French instrument. So, the board asked, why not an instrument designed locally?

Worst damaged of the train was this second class car, its side completely gouged out as it ran past the overturned engine and tender. Thirteen years later, this same carriage, reconstructed, was No. 2 behind the locomotive in the Tangiwai disaster. It was completely wrecked on that fateful Christmas Eve.

ISLINGTON 27 February 1946

More than a dozen trucks were wrecked when a big Ab engine drawing the fast express goods train from Dunedin rammed a stationary mixed train from the West Coast in the Islington railway yards at 6.30 a.m. on 27 February 1946.

Trucks and vans telescoped and climbed crazily on to one another in a scene of fantastic confusion. One particular pyramid of wood and metal was crowned by J wagons from which the corpses of sheep hung impaled on the splintered wreckage. Perhaps the most freakish result of the accident was a big Ub wagon, heavily laden with cement, which was next to the engine of the Dunedin train, driving right under the engine to force the rear bogies of the tender almost up to the cab. The superstructure of the next van was torn almost completely from the chassis and the contents spilt haphazardly along the track.

The scene in the Islington railway yards after the fog had lifted.

Passengers on the West Coast train escaped injury because the forepart of their train was shunting on another line, but the driver and fireman of the Dunedin train suffered shock and minor injuries.

'Conditions could not have been worse. It was so foggy you could not see a hand in front of you,' said Blenheim trainer R. Drinkwater. With other Riccarton trainers he was returning with his horses from the West Coast. 'Fortunately our train had been broken while sheep were shunted off and we were about a quarter of a mile away when the crash took place. The horses were thus untouched, but it was a cruel smash.'[1]

Cheeses, hogsheads of beer, smashed eggs, fruit, bottles, cases, piles of white yarn, machinery and many other items of the miscellany which made up a freight were strewn along the track. The station yard was heaped with this wild confusion of goods for some 45 m (50 yards) while coal freight from the West Coast was spread widely about the yard. Dead sheep also littered the wreckage.

BEYOND HUMAN CONTROL

LYTTELTON 26 March 1907

Instead of making the usual stately progress along the wharf to discharge passengers for the inter–island ferry at the usual point, locomotive R 28, about 6 p.m. on 26 March 1907, ran out of brakes, ploughed through a stop block and finished hanging perilously over the edge of the wharf.

Until that moment the procedure had been familiar — coupling up with the 'boat train' and trundling the carriages alongside the SS *Mararoa*. But when the crew came to apply the brakes it found, to its horror, that braking power to the carriages just did not exist.

The engine crossed the traverses, ploughed across the timber, knocked the rails beyond the traverses out of place, threw the stop block into the sea and plunged more than half its length over the end of the wharf. There it remained stationary, resting on the fire box bogie and four wheels. Cowcatcher, cylinders, driving and eccentric rods and all the gear under the boiler dropped into the sea.

Fortunately the design of the locomotive was similar to an articulated road transporter of today and was known in railway circles as Fairlie's Patent. The driving section was separate from the boiler, cab and coal bunker. This was the saving factor; otherwise one of Casey Jones' locomotives would have tumbled into Davy Jones' locker.

Nobody was injured when the train stopped with a terrific jerk, passengers tumbling out, much alarmed. When a diver went down the following day to recover the driving section, he found an La goods wagon which had been missing for a year.

Only centimetres from a watery grave at Lyttelton.

MATAROA 15 May 1919

Contemporary reports estimated a runaway goods train with a load of between 400 and 500 tonnes reached a speed of more than 150 km (100 miles) an hour shortly before it crashed at Mataroa, on the Ohakune-Taihape section of the Main Trunk line, in May 1919.

Locomotive X 592 and 32 wagons, including a guard's van, left Ohakune about 5 p.m. and the 25 km (16 miles) up a pretty stiff grade to Waiouru were negotiated safely. There was no difficulty in pulling up at Hihitahi, 12 km (8 miles) farther on, so that a crossing could be made with the Auckland-bound express, but on leaving Hihitahi, guard Batty became alarmed at the speed at which his train was travelling and the bumpy ride he was having as his guard's van negotiated the curves. He applied the Westinghouse brake in his van, but failed to get any response.

By now engine driver T. Welsh was keeping the whistle blowing erratically, an indication to the porter in charge of the Ngaurukehu station siding, which he was fast approaching, that the train was out of control and could not be pulled up. The train passed the station at a speed of more than 150 km (100 miles) an hour and, at a curve below the Ngaurukehu station, the engine shot off the track and the train was wrecked.

Goods piled up to an enormous height and huge wagons were smashed to matchwood. Timber, coal, butter boxes and wagon wheels were catapulted over the engine for more than 100 m ahead. Fireman J. McDonald managed to get out of the death trap, having ridden the engine to its end, along with the engine driver. Both suffered very severe scalding, the fireman's face being quite unrecognisable. The driver died after being extricated.

Locomotive X 592 where it flew off the track at Mataroa, showing the crumpled cab from which the driver had to be extricated by a relief working party from Taihape. He did not survive the accident.

Engine driver F. Westneath and fireman J. Reidy almost died when they were overcome by fumes in the Poro-o-tarao tunnel and their uncontrolled goods train crashed. Thirty head of cattle and 148 sheep were killed or had to be destroyed.

PORO-O-TARAO TUNNEL 30 July 1935

The longest tunnel in the North Island, the 1200 m (¾ mile) at Poro-o-tarao, almost killed engine driver F. Westneath and fireman J. Reidy on 30 July 1935.

The crew of a goods train proceeding north from Taumarunui, they collapsed in the tunnel and the train proceeded without control to crash into a samson block at the end of a dead line some 275 m (300 yds) from the mouth of the tunnel. Driver and fireman were extricated from the overturned engine dazed and suffering from shock, after the engine and 15 vehicles were derailed. Eight of the derailed wagons contained cattle and three contained sheep. Thirty head of cattle and 148 sheep were killed or had to be destroyed.

Porter in charge of the Poro-o-tarao station, H. Chote, had an on the spot view of the disaster. He was standing at the points south of the station at 1.55 a.m., waiting for the arrival of the goods train which left Taumarunui at 11.10. The train consisted of an Aa engine and 46 vehicles. The signal was against it, for it was supposed to be sidetracked to Poro-o-tarao so that the Huntly coal train, which was nearly due from the north, could be sidetracked and so that the northbound express could pass.

When the Taumarunui runaway train emerged from the tunnel, porter Chote became alarmed because, instead of pulling up, the train proceeded north at a high and increasing rate of speed. Two stationary empty trucks were on the dead end line and were crashed into and driven before the runaway. The samson block at the end of the siding stopped the errant train, but the impetus carried the engine and 15 of the wagons behind it to a point eight truck lengths beyond the stopper block. The engine fell down a small embankment and turned upside down, with many of the trucks derailed together in a heap and reduced to matchwood.

Guard H. McQuillan, accompanied by drovers travelling with him in the van, did not at first suspect the nature of the accident, the first part of train having broken away from the remainder. The drovers and the guard went to help the engine driver and fireman, both of whom were found unconscious, huddled in the cab of the engine, over which the tender was telescoped. The driving wheels of the engine were still running, the throttle being open, and the cab was enveloped in steam. The two men were taken out of the cab through the ventilator at the top and carried to the station.

Both men recovered and did not seem much the worse for their experience. Driver Westneath remembered nothing from the time he became suffocated with smoke fumes in the tunnel until he recovered consciousness at the station. Fireman Reidy was not aware of the engine driver's collapse in the tunnel because it was pitch dark. He lost consciousness. Just before the crash he became conscious and, realising the danger, attempted to apply the Westinghouse brake. He was too late, the crash happened, and he again lost consciousness.

The engine was extensively damaged and most of the wrecked wagons were smashed beyond repair, but the train crew was alive and uninjured, after an appalling experience.

WHANGAEHU RIVER 1941

Some years before the deviation of the Wanganui-Marton line between Okoia and Turakina, the old line after leaving Okoia ascended a very steep grade to Fordell (the summit) and then descended a very long winding steep grade to pass through the Whangaehu Valley, climbing again to pass over the Ratana flat.

On the night Ab 661 engine driver MacLauchlan and fireman Benefield were thrown off the rails into the Whangaehu River, the train from Wanganui to Marton had left Fordell. This night goods was drifting down the steep gradient and was nearing the point were the railway crosses the main highway (before realignment), very near the north end of the Whangaehu railway bridge.

Unbeknown to the train crew, a goods wagon had become derailed while the train was descending the steep grade, but because the buffers did not break, and because the rear of the train concertinaed towards the forward wagons, the derailed wagon kept on a running course until the derailed wheels struck the check rails on the cattle stops on each side of the main highway, thereby carrying other wagons off the rails. By this time Ab 661 was on the north approach of the bridge, where another set of check rails sent the derailed wagons askew and into the river, hauling the engine and tender with them.

The train crew survived the accident after a considerable time trapped in the river, but lady luck was near at hand. Dr Church was returning to Marton from Wanganui at a very early hour and noticed the wreckage. He immediately investigated and gave first aid, although it was some time before the engine crew was relieved.

The Whangaehu River has certainly been unkind to Railways personnel. According to *Railway Station Names and Their Meanings* (Publicity Branch, New Zealand Railways,

Wellington, 1936), the Maori explanation of Whangaehu is: 'whango', bay, or mouth of river; 'ehu', turbid. The water of the Whangaehu sometimes has a discoloured appearance, caused by its sulphurous origin on Mount Ruapehu. The turbid nature of the river was shown in 1953, in the Tangiwai disaster.

Locomotive Ab 661, 6 m (20 ft) below the viaduct which crossed the river on the Marton to Wanganui line in 1941. Good fortune saved the train crew.

ELLERSLIE 4 January 1943

When the leading bogie left the rails as the train was approaching the Ellerslie Railway Station on 4 January 1943, the lead engine of the Auckland to Papakura train struck the stone support of the overhead bridge on the left side and caused the bridge to collapse on the engine.

The front bogies of the engine had left the track completely and the front wheels of the leading car were also derailed, but only one passenger suffered any injury, in his case slight scratches. The left side of the engine was fairly extensively damaged and the platforms of the first and second of the six carriages were smashed. The gas main carried by the overhead bridge was damaged but leaks were quickly blocked by a repair gang.

Derailed Wab 769 and the derailed front carriage of the Auckland–Papakura train at Ellerslie, with the collapsed footbridge straddling the engine.

A pig crossing the track caused the derailment of an engine near Hukarere.

Chapter 6

ANIMAL VICTIMS

Railway accidents involving trains carrying livestock too often present a distressing conclusion — dead animals, maimed animals which have to be shot and the occasional maniac beast, crazed by fear, which runs amok and has to be cornered before being shot, usually in a most public place.

MANGAROA 9 April 1900

Half a consignment of 2800 sheep in a train wrecked between Kaitoke and Mangaroa on 9 April 1900 were killed or mutilated, with many having to be killed by having their throats cut because of injury.

The train consisted of 40 sheep trucks, eight timber, four goods trucks and two guards' vans, plus a brake van in the middle and another at the end.

The accident happened when one of the trucks in the middle of the train veered off the rails and bumped along until reaching an embankment curve where the grade was 1 in 46. There some of the trucks went over on to their side and those behind telescoped on to them. The shock broke the engine couplings and saved the engine. The guard at the rear of the train succeeded in putting brakes on, to save his van and four timber trucks, but the rest piled up on each side of the bank, or on the line itself to form a pyramid 6–7.5 m high.

Brakesman Hicks, in the middle van, had his left arm crushed to pulp, his left leg broken and his face cut and bruised. Rescuers took two hours to extricate him.

The cost of this accident was estimated to be more than £7,000, made up of each truck being worth £100, the vans £200 each and the sheep at least 12/-.

HUKARERE 1920s

Engine driver G. Stevens and his fireman, J. Mahon, were making only a steady pace with a mixed train near Hukarere on the West Coast of the South Island in the 1920s when a pig crossing the track threw their engine off the rails and into long grass beside the track. The locomotive was N 30.

GORE 12 June 1946

A J class engine and seven wagons of the Invercargill to Dunedin night goods train were derailed when the engine struck a bullock wandering on the line about 275 m (300 yds) south of the Gore Borough boundary just before midnight on 12 June 1946.

The train was travelling about 40 km (26 miles) an hour when it ran into a herd of 40 cattle as it approached Gore. The engine struck a bullock, which the driver said afterwards seemed to pass under the wheels. The impact caused the light trucks between the engine and the remainder of the train to buck into the air and fly off the rails, two to the right, five to the left of the main line.

The engine carried on for about 90 m (100 yds), throwing the mauled carcase of the bullock clear, then slewed round to the right. The nose of the engine ploughed to the depth of the boiler into the clay at the side of the line, while the cab buckled between the angle of the engine and the tender.

The only injury suffered by the driver was a cut on the hand, received when he escaped through the window. The fireman also managed to get clear almost unhurt.

CHAPTER 7

THE END OF THE LINE

Derailed while shunting a rake of loaded trucks on a siding in heavy fog at Westfield in the early hours of an April morning in 1953, the 140 tonne locomotive K 901 came to rest straddling a concrete stop block. The engine finished down a 2.5 m (8 ft) bank with the front bogie 7.5 m (25 ft) from the end of the line.

It was a temporary end of the line for K 901, which was pulled back on to the tracks after a temporary line had been built beneath it and the engine went back into service. K 901 was retired in 1964 along with 23 locomotives of the same class and 77 steam locomotives overall.

Locomotive K 901 derailed at Westfield in April 1953. The words chalked on the tender of the engine referred to the racehorse Jon Rosa, which raced under the colours of the then Minister of Railways, the Hon. W. S. Goosman.

But, if not immediately for K 901, 1952 marked the official beginning of the end of the line for steam power on New Zealand railway tracks. The next few years were what has been described as the twilight period for steam railway power, as engines were phased out after the adoption of a dieselisation policy in 1952.

The very first hint of change came with the opening in 1923 of New Zealand's first electrified railway between Otira and Arthur's Pass, running for a distance of 12.5 km (8 miles) and passing through the 8.5 km (5¼ miles) just-completed Otira Tunnel on a grade of 1 in 33 throughout. This combination excluded the use of steam locomotives.

Piecemeal electrification development was carried out until the Wellington-Paekakariki section of the North Island Main Trunk railway was coverted in 1940. Now, electrification is departmental policy, with significant development on the Main Trunk through the central North Island well under way.

Diesel traction was introduced in 1936 with railcars on the Wellington-Wairarapa route. The cars were specially designed for service on the steep grade of the Rimutaka incline. Diesel-mechanical shunting locomotives appeared in 1949, followed by main line diesel-electric locomotives.

On the eve of the beginning of the changeover proper, about 1950, New Zealand's steam locomotives consumed on average 50 kg (1 cwt) of coal a mile — 30 kg a kilometre — and in a year burnt more than 500,000 tonnes of coal and 86 million litres (19 m gallons) of fuel oil. From that majestic parade of Ja's, the Wab, the K family and the A's, Ab's and so on — in 1950 there were 627 steam locomotives of 28 different classes in service on New Zealand Railways — the rundown has been complete. The only locomotives in departmental service in New Zealand today are the two Ab class engines used on the Kingston Flyer tourist train.

In the debate between straightout electrification and diesel-electrification, much has been made of cost factors — the cost of imported diesel fuel as against hydro-electricity or New Zealand based oil fire generating stations; the relative advantages of the two types of engines, diesel being the dearer with a notably shorter working life; the high initial capital cost of overhead gantries and substations for the electric system. But the 1949 departmental commission appointed to report on future motive power came down wholeheartedly for electrification. Steam had had its day.

The commission found that electric units were clean and easy to operate, against the steam engine's inherent dirtiness. The time taken out for boiler washouts and overhaul compared with only rotating gear in the electric counterparts. The electric engine had greater mechanical efficiency; steam had very low thermal efficiency.

So New Zealand is in the process of converting to electrification and, where electrification is awaited, making do with diesel-electric power. But spare a thought for the years of steam trains in New Zealand, in spite of their very occasional horrendous accidents. For the rest there was the full-throated blast of the steam train whistle, steam hissing between side rods and valve gear and smoke trailing luxuriously back over the train, a long white-grey plume crowning the glory which was a steam express at full bore, imperious in its dignity, exciting, moving. And it is all now a part of history, along with the steam engine accident toll recounted in these pages.

APPENDICES

TEXT REFERENCES

CHAPTER 1 TANGIWAI: TRAGEDY THAT STUNNED A NATION

1. NZPA 25 December 1953.
2. Graham Stewart. *Tangiwai Disaster and 30 Other Railway Accidents in New Zealand,* Wilson & Horton, Auckland, 1972, p. 7.
3. *Ibid.*
4. NZPA 27 December 1953.
5. *Ibid.*, 25 December 1953.
6. *Ibid.*, 27 December 1953.
7. *Ibid.*
8. *Ibid.*
9. *Ibid.*
10. *Ibid.*, 23 December 1953.
11. NZPA 25 December 1953.
12. *Ibid.*
13. *Ibid.*
14. NZPA 3 March 1954.
15. *Ibid.*, 1 March 1954.
16. *Ibid.*, 25 December 1953.
17. *Ibid.*
18. *Ibid.*
19. NZPA 25 December 1953.
20. *Ibid.*
21. *ibid.*
22. *The Press,* Christchurch, 25 December 1953.
23. *Ibid.*
24. NZPA, London, 26 December 1953.
25. *Ibid.*, 27 December 1953.
26. NZPA 4 January 1954.
27. *Ibid.*, 31 December 1953.
28. *Ibid.*, 29 December 1953.

Board of Inquiry

1. NZPA 2 March 1954.
2. *Ibid.*, 3 March 1954.
3. *Ibid.*, 2 March 1954.
4. *Ibid.*
5. *Ibid.*
6. *Ibid.*
7. *Ibid.*, 9 March 1954.
8. *Ibid.*, 10 March 1954.
9. Transcript of evidence, p. 4. (Graham Stewart papers)
10. *Ibid.*, p. 7.
11. NZPA 12 March 1954.
12. *Ibid.*, 9 March 1954.
13. NZPA 12 March 1954.
14. Transcript, p. 6Q-1.
15. *Ibid.*, p. 6L-2.
16. *Ibid.*
17. *Ibid.*, p. 6M-3.
18. NZPA 8 March 1954.
19. *Ibid.*
20. *Ibid.*, 12 March 1954.
21. *Ibid.*, 1 April 1954.
22. Board of inquiry report, p. 17.
23. *Ibid.*
24. *Ibid.*, p. 7–8.
25. *Ibid.*, p. 21.
26. *Ibid.*, p. 23.
27. *Ibid.*, p. 24.
28. *Ibid.*

CHAPTER 2 THE 10 WORST AFTER TANGIWAI

1. *Board of inquiry report, 'Derailment of Passenger Train between Haywards and Andrews Stations', 1943, p. 8.*
2. *Board of inquiry report, 'Derailment of Special Excursion Train near Ratana on 26th March 1938', 1938, p. 11.*

Rimutaka Incline

1. *New Zealand Herald,* 14 September 1880.

Rakaia

1. *New Zealand Herald,* 21 March 1899.

Whangamarino

1. *New Zealand Herald,* 11 June 1914.
2. *Ibid.*, 28 May 1914.
3. *Ibid.*
4. *Ibid.*, 13 June 1914.
5. *Ibid.*, 16 June 1914.
6. *Ibid.*

Ongarue

1. *New Zealand Herald,* 9 July 1923.
2. *Ibid.*, 7 July 1923.
3. *Ibid.*, 9 July 1923.
4. *Ibid.*, 10 July 1923.
5. *Ibid.*, 9 July 1923.
6. *Ibid.*, 7 July 1923.
7. *Ibid.*
8. *Ibid.*, 9 July 1923.
9. *Ibid.*, 7 July 1923.
10. *Ibid.*, 9 July 1923.
11. *Ibid.*
12. Annual Report, New Zealand Railways, 1924, D-2, p. xviii.
13. D. A. Bathgate. *Doctor in the Sticks,* Collins, 1972, p. 140.

Opapa

1. *New Zealand Herald,* 23 September 1925.
2. NZPA 23 September 1925.

Ratana

1. Board of inquiry report, 'Derailment of Special Excursion Train near Ratana on 26th March 1938', I–D. 3. p. 11.
2. *New Zealand Herald,* 28 March 1938.
3. Board of inquiry report, p. 12.
4. *Ibid.*

Hyde

1. *New Zealand Herald,* 5 June 1943.
2. Board of inquiry, 'Hyde Railway Accident', p. 9.
3. *Ibid.*, p. 1.

Haywards

1. Board of inquiry report, 'Derailment of Passenger Train between Haywards and Andrews Stations, 23rd December 1943', p. 9.
2. *Ibid.*, p. 12.
3. *Ibid.*, p. 13.

Seddon
1. *Evening Post*, 13 April 1948.
2. Board of inquiry report, 'Accident to Picton–Christchurch Express Train between Seddon and Blind River Stations, 25th February 1948', p. 8.
3. *The Southern Cross*, 10 July 1948.
4. *Evening Post*, 19 May 1948.
5. *Ibid.*, 2 April 1948.
6. *Ibid.*
7. *Ibid.*, 13 April 1948.
8. *Ibid.*
9. *New Zealand Herald*, 26 February 1948.

CHAPTER 3 A PERILOUS LANDSCAPE

Chaneys
1. *New Zealand Herald*, 27 June 1905.

Taringamotu
1. *New Zealand Herald*, 26 July 1915.
2. *Ibid.*

Kakahi
1. *New Zealand Herald*, 26 May 1925.

Paraparaumu
1. *New Zealand Herald*, 31 August 1936.
2. *Ibid.*
3. *Ibid.*

Raurimu
1. *New Zealand Herald*, 8 January 1945.
2. *Ibid.*

Hihitahi
1. *The Daily Telegraph*, 8 July 1961.
2. *Ibid.*
3. *Ibid.*, 10 July 1961.
4. *Ibid.*, 8 July 1961.

CHAPTER 4 SEMAPHORE ARM TO CTC
1. *Appendices to the Journal of the House of Representatives*, H-14 of A to J, p. 2–4.
2. C. R. Lovatt paper, 'Modern Railway Signalling: New Zealand Railways', 24 March 1949, A. C. Bellamy papers, p. 4.
3. *Ibid.*, p. 5.

Bankside
1. NZPA 30 March 1907.

New Lynn
1. *New Zealand Herald*, 29 May 1913.

Papatoetoe
1. *New Zealand Herald*, 26 August 1946.
2. *Ibid.*
3. *The Daily Telegraph*, 22 February 1947.

Levin
1. *The Daily Telegraph*, 13 April 1950.
2. *Ibid.*
3. *Ibid.*, 7 June 1950.
4. *Ibid.*
5. *Evening Post*, 11 July 1950.

CHAPTER 5 MANNING THE SYSTEM
1. *The Daily Telegraph*, 24 January 1961.

Mamaku Incline
1. *New Zealand Herald*, 3 August 1907.
2. *Ibid.*, 5 August 1907.
3. *Ibid.*, 29 August 1907.
4. *Ibid.*, 31 August 1907.
5. Report on Rotorua Railway Accident Inquiry, 1907, D-7, p. 2.

Mercer
1. Board of inquiry report, 'Mercer Railway Accident', p. 12.
2. *Ibid.*

Islington
1. *Christchurch Star Sun*, 27 February 1946.

BIBLIOGRAPHY

NEWSPAPERS:

New Zealand Herald, Auckland.
Auckland Star.
Evening Post, Wellington.
The Press, Christchurch.
Christchurch Star-Sun.
Otago Daily Times, Dunedin.
The Daily Telegraph, Napier.
Nelson Evening Mail.
New Zealand Truth, Wellington.

PAPER:

Lovatt, C. R. 'Modern Railway Signalling: New Zealand Railways', 1949. A. C. Bellamy papers.

BOOKS:

Bathgate, D. A. *Doctor in the Sticks*, Collins, 1972.
Cooke, John & Vogel, John. *New Zealand Steam Finale*, Collins, 1979.
'Cross at Rakaia! The Fatal Collision of 11 March 1899', Canterbury branch, New Zealand Railway and Locomotive Society, undated.
McGavin, T. A. *Steam Locomotives of New Zealand Railways*, the New Zealand Railway and Locomotive Society, 1950.
Mulgan, A. *New Zealand Railways: Romance and Story*, reprinted from *New Zealand Geographer*, Vol. 10, No. 1, April 1954.
New Zealand Year Book, Government Printer, 1985.
Publicity and Advertising branch, New Zealand Railways Wellington. 'The Growth of New Zealand Railways', undated.
'Our Railways: New Zealand's National Transport Service', 1961.
Stewart, Graham. *Tangiwai Disaster and Thirty Other Railway Accidents in New Zealand*, Wilson and Horton Ltd., 1972.
The New Zealand Railways Magazine.
Troup, Gordon, ed. *Steel Roads of New Zealand: An Illustrated Survey*, A.H. & A.W. Reed, Wellington, 1973.

THE EIGHTH WORST

With a death roll of 151, the Tangiwai rail disaster, at the time it happened, was rated the eighth worst in the world by the toll of those killed and injured.
The most serious railway accidents until 1953 were:

1864, 29 June, near Beloeil, Canada. Train ran through open switch. 90 killed.

1879, 28 December, Dundee, Scotland. Train blown off Tay bridge. 73 drowned.

1881, 24 June, near Cuartla, Mexico. Train fell into river. About 200 died.

1882, 13 July, near Tcherny, Russia. Train derailed. More than 150 killed.

1889, 12 June, near Armagh, Ireland. Collision. About 80 killed.

1891, 14 June, near Basel, Switzerland. Collision. About 100 killed.

1904, 7 August, Eden, Colorado. Two-train collision. 96 killed.

1910, 1 March, Wellington, Washington, USA. Two trains swept into canyon by avalanche. 96 killed.

1915, 22 May, Gretna, Scotland. Two passenger trains and a troop train collided. 227 killed.

1917, 12 December, Modane, France. Troop train derailed. Almost 550 killed.

1918, 1 November, New York city. Derailment. 92 killed.

1939, 22 November, near Magdeburg, Germany. Collision. 200 killed.

1943, 16 December, near Rennert, North Carolina, USA. Derailment. 72 killed.

1944, 2 March, near Salerno, Italy. Train stalled in tunnel. 521 suffocated.

1949, 22 October, near Nowy Dwor, Poland. Derailment of Danzig-Warsaw express. 200 killed.

1950, 22 November, Richmond Hill, New York. Commuter train crashed into rear of another. 79 killed.

1951, 6 February, Woodbridge, New Jersey, USA. Commuter train plunged through temporary overpass. 85 killed.

1952, 8 October, Harrow-Wealdstone, England. Two express trains crash into commuter train. 112 killed.

1953, 24 December, Tangiwai, New Zealand. Lahar sweeps train from bridge. 151 killed.

1953, 24 December, near Sakvice, Czechoslovakia. Two trains crashed. More than 100 killed.

Other Grantham House Illustrated Histories

NEW ZEALAND TRAGEDIES
Shipwrecks and Maritime Disasters
Gavin McLean

Stories of terrifying storms, of inhospitable coastlines, of human error, of the malicious hand of fate. Also testimonies to tremendous courage and endurance. More than 200 superb photographs help bring alive the dramatic events of New Zealand's seafaring past.

PORTRAIT OF THE ROYAL NEW ZEALAND NAVY
A Fiftieth Anniversary Celebration
Grant Howard. Paintings by Colin Wynn

Fifty colour plates of the naval ships which have served New Zealand. The book traces the part played by the Navy since the arrival of Lieutenant James Cook, RN, in HMS *Endeavour* in 1769. Black and white photographs of human interest complete the story.

PORTRAIT OF AN AIR FORCE
The Royal New Zealand Air Force
Geoffrey Bentley and Maurice Conly

A celebration of RNZAF aircraft, squadrons and personnel – a timely tribute to our Air Force. 28 full-colour oil paintings, 73 charcoal drawings and over 200 photographs.

SILVER WINGS
The Story of New Zealand Women Aviators
Shirley Laine

An overdue recognition of the role of women in New Zealand aviation. Shirley Laine, a pilot herself, supports her story from the pioneer era to the present with a remarkable collection of photographs of women flyers, parachutists, skydivers, gliders and aircraft.

WHEN TRAMS WERE TRUMPS IN NEW ZEALAND
Graham Stewart

Suburban travel before the motorcar. New Zealanders rode them to school, to work, to sports and many to fame. A pictorial parade of these classic vehicles through the changing facades of streets in our cities, spanning more than 100 years.